ENDORSEMENTS

Candice Smithyman has been a great encouragement to me in understanding times and seasons. In *Cracking the Time Code,* she invites us to live our lives from the faith realm of being seated in heavenly places where eternal time frees us from the dominion of our earthly anxiety. This is not a mere self-help book but an invitation into meditation, revelation, and ascendancy into the winged life.

Lou Engle
Founder, Lou Engle Ministries

Candice Smithyman has written a beautiful, insightful, and practical guide to understanding and overcoming the season believers currently live in. Time and timing can either be a difficult barrier, a stumbling block, or a doorway into the power and eternal purposes of God—depending on our interaction with Him. I believe reading this book will be an eye-opening and intellectually expanding experience for most Christians today. You can walk in all God has provided for you now, not in some foggy future. Read this book and do what she has suggested, and I believe your whole experience in Jesus will be transformed.

Joan Hunter
Evangelist, Author
Host, *Miracles Happen* TV show

Time is not your enemy, but your perception of it could hold you back in ways you can't imagine. *Cracking the Time Code* exposes one of the greatest deceptions plaguing believers today: the idea that we are still bound by the curse of time. Through fresh revelation and powerful scriptural insight, Candice Smithyman pulls back the veil and invites us to step into what Jesus actually purchased for us. This book carries an anointing to break cycles of delay, defeat the toiling mindset, and recalibrate your entire worldview. You'll walk away from reading this book realizing you're not behind—you're right on time! If you've ever felt like the clock is working against you, *Cracking the Time Code* is your call to redemption, restoration, and supernatural acceleration.

Alan DiDio
Pastor, The Encounter Charlotte
Host of *Encounter Today*

This book is no ordinary work, but one anointed with fresh revelation in regard to God's eternal time. Candice has given us a fresh insight into this revelation and carries tremendous love and grace on her life! I highly recommend this book and believe you will receive an impartation of this revelation as you read.

Pastor Cyndy Mooring
Celebration of Life Church
Baytown, Texas

With each turn of the page of *Cracking the Time Code,* your eyes and ears of faith will be opened as Candice unpacks rich truth from the Word. You will feel her right there beside you cheering you on as she leads you through each activation. Get ready for the shift because you are being positioned to receive all the benefits Jesus died to give you.

Susan Cheatham Ministries
Worship Leader, Chaplain
Author, *Unlock Your Inheritance Devotionals* and *Prosper in God's Appointed Times and Seasons*
SCMfire.org

Cracking the Time Code is a profound invitation to break free from the limitations of earthly time, breaking free of the curse of lack and delay! Candice will equip you to experience supernatural acceleration, purpose, and peace!

Jenny Donnelly
Founder, Her Voice Movement
#DontMessWithOurKidS

When Jesus appeared on the scene, He began His earthly ministry with a declaration: *"Repent, for the kingdom of heaven is at hand!"* (Matthew 3:2 NKJV). The Greek word for repentance, *metanoia*, involves more than just turning away from sin; it means to completely change your thinking—to do a transformative paradigm shift. In her new book, Candice Smithyman, a commissioned HIM apostle and faculty member of Wagner University, imparts catalytic keys to experiencing Kingdom paradigm shifts in your life. *Cracking the Time Code* is accessible, edifying, and ultimately reformational in its framework. It will uniquely set you up to bring Heaven's Kingdom to earth and be a change agent for God's eternal glory. Wow, what a book!

Dr. Ché Ahn
Senior Leader, Harvest Rock Church, Pasadena, CA
President, Harvest International Ministry
International Chancellor, Wagner University

Once again I find myself drinking at the same firehose of Revelation that my dear friend Candice is. The governance of the created realm is what those made in the image and likeness of God were called to, as our first mandate! The next great restorative revelation, right now, is our ability to govern time! When Candice and I were revelating a while back and she began sharing what God was showing her about time governance, it was at that time when God was sharing with me about Galatians 5:16 and redeeming the *time* for the days are evil! All of creation is groaning, waiting for the manifestation of the children of God! The whole world is waiting for the mature children to understand: Who He (God) is; Whose we are; and Who we are! We are the Ecclesia, the governors, and that includes time! You are no longer subjected to time. Time is not your taskmaster! My desire is for you to generously receive this book as a portal to open up your limitless potential! This book will enable you to take a quantum leap from mere linear thinking to a supersonic light speed of dimensional living!

Bishop Barry C. Maracle
Author, *Wake Up Into Your Dream*
Founder, Take Charge Ministries
Founder, Ascent the Summit Leadership Experience

Cracking the Time Code is a revelatory journey into the heart of eternity that may possibly challenge everything you thought you understood about time and your divine inheritance in Christ. Dr. Candice Smithyman has blessed the body of Christ with a prophetic blueprint for stepping into supernatural acceleration, breaking cycles of delay, and accessing Heaven's agenda in the now. With bold insight and spiritual authority, Dr. Smithyman takes the reader beyond the veil—into realms of heavenly time where miracles flow, destinies are unlocked, and the toiling of earth time is exchanged for the rest of eternal living. This book doesn't just inspire—it equips. Each chapter unfolds a key that will help you transcend the limitations of chronos and begin living from kairos, from the throne room of God Himself.

If you are tired of striving, if you sense the divine call to walk in the fullness of what Jesus purchased for you—not someday, but today—this book is your invitation. Prepare to be awakened, stretched, and positioned to live from the eternal realm, bringing Heaven to earth in every step.

Dr. Joshua Fowler
Author, *The Five Porches*
Apostle, AwakeTheWorld.org
Panama City Beach, Florida

Dr. Candice is a brilliant teacher and preacher of God's Word. Her command and knowledge of the Scripture is sound in doctrine and transformative to all her readers. But what motivates me to read her books is the life-changing revelation that flows in and through her. The wisdom keys on the pages of this book are going to change your paradigm, delivering you from limiting beliefs as it relates to all things connected to harvest and time. You will learn that you are from another Kingdom, and God has heavenly strategies and codes for living a supernatural life every day of your natural life here on earth.

Pastor Callie Gray
Celebration of Life Church
Baytown, Texas

CRACKING THE TIME CODE

Destiny Image Books By Candice Smithyman

365 Prophetic Revelations from the Hebrew Calendar: Experience the Power, Blessing, and Abundance of Aligning with God's Times and Seasons

Releasing Heaven's Atmosphere into Chaos, Crisis, and Fear

Angels of Fire: The Ministry of Angels in End-Time Revival

Releasing Heaven: Creating a Supernatural Environment Through Heavenly Encounters

Cracking the Time Code: Step Into Supernatural Acceleration, Stop Cycles of Delay, and Secure God's Promises Today

CANDICE SMITHYMAN

CRACKING THE TIME CODE

STEP INTO SUPERNATURAL ACCELERATION, STOP CYCLES OF DELAY, AND SECURE GOD'S PROMISES TODAY

DESTINY IMAGE® PUBLISHERS, INC.
P.O. Box 310, Shippensburg, PA 17257-0310
"Publishing cutting-edge prophetic resources to supernaturally empower the body of Christ"

This book and all other Destiny Image and Destiny Image Fiction books are available at Christian bookstores and distributors worldwide.

For more information on foreign distributors, call 717-532-3040.
Reach us on the Internet: www.destinyimage.com.

ISBN 13 TP: 979-8-8815-0538-7
ISBN 13 eBook: 979-8-8815-0539-4
ISBN 13 HC: 979-8-8815-0541-7
ISBN 13 LP: 979-8-8815-0542-4

For Worldwide Distribution, Printed in the U.S.A.
1 2 3 4 5 6 7 8 / 30 29 28 27 26

DEDICATION

*This book is dedicated to my beloved mother,
Joan Marie Farhood Borland Rainsberger, who is now experiencing
the fullness of eternal time in spirit, soul, and body.*

ACKNOWLEDGMENTS

First, I am thankful to my Lord and Savior Jesus Christ who has entrusted me with this revelation of eternal time to share with others.

I thank my family for their sacrifice and encouragement in all of my book writing and their patience in my time spent away as I travel to carry the message of the gospel. The top of the list is my beloved husband, Adam Smithyman, for his faithfulness to care so much for our family while I am writing and traveling.

My daughter, Alexandria, who brings to life through media the teachings of the *Glory Road* TV show and for the years she has traveled globally with me.

My daughter, Samantha, who carries out the administration of Dream Mentors and holds credentialing classes for leaders worldwide, and son-in-law Hunter who tirelessly encourages Sammi and is a great dad to our three granddaughters: Lily, Leighton, and Everly.

My son, Nicholas, and daughter-in-law, Avery, and grandbabies, Asher and Addy, who have partnered with the ministry for many years to help us bring the revelation of the Kingdom to those in need.

My faithful sister and brother-in-law, Debra and Rob Hodgson.

Prayer is at the center of this ministry, so big thanks to my intercessory team, overseen by Maria DiSebastiano, and for many years with faithful intercessors Elisa Andrews and Shilove Jean-Baptiste, and the team that is growing.

Our Dream Mentors ministry affiliates and network coaches who continue to take the messages we teach at Dream Mentors to the body of Christ all around the world.

My *Glory Road* TV partners and ASCEND class members who allow me to pour the revelation of the Kingdom and eternal realms into their lives.

The team at Destiny Image of Larry Sparks and Tina Pugh, and the production/editorial staff of Shaun Tabatt, Katie Rios, and graphic artist Eileen Rockwell, who always does amazing covers for my books.

My producer Connie Janzen, of Your Path to Destiny on It's Supernatural Network (ISN), and Marian Duffee who help through prayer and taking these messages into global media.

There are so many others to acknowledge and thank for their time and encouragement—the list is too long to share.

CONTENTS

CONTENTS

FOREWORD

BY TROY A. BREWER

There are very few people who carry the presence of the Lord with such elegance and authority as my friend, Dr. Candice Smithyman. She is a woman of wisdom, fierce in the Spirit, compassionate in heart, and relentless in her pursuit of the Kingdom of God. You don't meet too many people in life who are truly what I call "drop-dead-sold-out-Jesus-freaks." But when you do, your life is better for it.

Candice is the real deal. Period.

She's not only an apostle and minister, she's also a teacher and a deeply prophetic voice to the body of Christ. I've had the honor of doing ministry alongside her and seeing firsthand her sensitivity to the Holy Spirit, her boldness in truth, and her unshakable devotion to Jesus. She doesn't just preach messages, she lives them. She walks the walk, and she walks it well.

Now, let me tell you something personal. Candice has been a prophetic voice in *my* life who has been accurate, timely, and always pointing back to Jesus. There have been moments when I've needed a word from Heaven, and God used Candice to speak clarity, direction, and hope. You can't buy that kind of authenticity or spiritual integrity. It's rare. It's refined. And it's completely Holy Ghost.

What she brings in this book, *Cracking the Time Code*, is not just another teaching, it's a revelation. This is a Kingdom download, straight from the eternal realms, and it's delivered with power and grace. This book will open your eyes to a supernatural way of seeing time, not as a thief, but as something already redeemed by Jesus Himself.

Candice invites you to step into the everlasting zone where time bends to Kingdom purpose, where delay is destroyed, and where acceleration by the Spirit becomes your new normal. This isn't just poetic language or inspirational fluff. This is hard-hitting, biblically anchored truth that will shift your thinking and launch you into new realms of faith and favor.

I'm especially grateful for how Candice approaches life and ministry with an open hand and a generous heart. She has personally sown into our mission to rescue children out of sexual trafficking, and I mean truly *sown*. Not just financially, though she's been faithful in that. She's sown with her prayers, her voice, her influence, and her platform. That kind of Kingdom generosity doesn't go unnoticed, and I honor her for it.

We need more people like Candice Smithyman, people who seek the heart of God above all else and aren't afraid to break religious norms to release Heaven on earth. People who burn with the fire of the Holy Ghost and still have the humility to sit at the feet of Jesus.

Friend, as you read this book, I encourage you to open your heart wide. Don't just read it with your head but read it with your spirit too. Let the Holy Spirit reveal truths to you that have been hidden in plain sight. Let your soul be unlocked from the chains of fear, time anxiety, and small thinking. Let this message catapult you into a fresh understanding of God's timing, God's provision, and God's eternal plan for your life.

Candice isn't just handing you keys to revelation, she's handing you a blueprint for supernatural living in the here and now.

I'm honored to call her a friend. I'm honored to run with her in the Kingdom. And I'm thankful—truly thankful—that I get to do life with a sister in Christ who's laid down everything for the cause of Jesus.

So, buckle up. Get ready. You're about to crack the time code—and once you do, there's no going back.

Let's go,

Troy A. Brewer
Senior Pastor, OpenDoor Church
Founder, Troy Brewer Ministries

INTRODUCTION

In Matthew 27:45-66 (KJV), the revelation of *Cracking the Time Code* exists. This time code was "cracked" in the very beginning in Genesis 3, when the curse of the fall of man happened. The "cracked time code" exists today within our earthly time zone, which is made up of a cycle of night and day (Genesis 1:5).

Let us begin our journey of learning to "crack the time code" every day of our lives by what we choose to believe about the death, burial, resurrection, and ascension of Jesus. The story begins here in the ninth hour or 3:00 p.m. This is why the cover of this book shows a watch with the time set on the ninth hour or 3:00 p.m.

> Now from the sixth hour there was darkness over all the land unto the ***ninth hour.*** And ***about the ninth hour*** Jesus cried with a loud voice, saying, Eli, Eli, lama sabachthani? that is to say, My God, my God, why hast thou forsaken me? Some of them that stood there, when they heard that, said, This man calleth for Elias. And straightway one of them ran, and took a spunge, and

filled it with vinegar, and put it on a reed, and gave him to drink. The rest said, Let be, let us see whether Elias will come to save him. Jesus, when he had cried again with a loud voice, yielded up the ghost.

And, behold, the veil of the temple was rent in twain from the top to the bottom; and the earth did quake, and the rocks rent; And the graves were opened; and many bodies of the saints which slept arose, And came out of the graves after his resurrection, and went into the holy city, and appeared unto many. Now when the centurion, and they that were with him, watching Jesus, saw the earthquake, and those things that were done, they feared greatly, saying, Truly this was the Son of God.

And many women were there beholding afar off, which followed Jesus from Galilee, ministering unto him: Among which was Mary Magdalene, and Mary the mother of James and Joses, and the mother of Zebedees children. When the even was come, there came a rich man of Arimathaea, named Joseph, who also himself was Jesus' disciple: He went to Pilate, and begged the body of Jesus. Then Pilate commanded the body to be delivered. And when Joseph had taken the body, he wrapped it in a clean linen cloth, And laid it in his own new tomb, which he had hewn out in the rock: and he rolled a great stone to the door of the sepulchre, and departed. And there was Mary Magdalene, and the other Mary, sitting over against the sepulchre.

Now the next day, that followed the day of the preparation, the chief priests and Pharisees came together unto Pilate, Saying, Sir, we remember that that deceiver said, while he was yet alive, ***After three days I will rise again.*** Command therefore that the sepulchre be

> made sure until ***the third day***, lest his disciples come by night, and steal him away, and say unto the people, He is risen from the dead: so the last error shall be worse than the first. Pilate said unto them, Ye have a watch: go your way, make it as sure as ye can. So they went, and made the sepulchre sure, sealing the stone, and ***setting a watch*** (Matthew 27:48-66 KJV).

At Jesus's death at the ninth hour, which is 3:00 p.m. in the afternoon Israel time, the veil was rent (torn) from top to bottom and access to the Holy of Holies in the heavenly tabernacle was made available to us all. At the ninth hour, or 3:00 p.m., our High Priest, Jesus Christ, the Son of the living God, met all the requirements of the Mosaic Law in regard to the earthly tabernacle, and put His blood on the mercy seat in the ark of the covenant in the heavenly tabernacle on the Day of Atonement and declared, "It is finished."

Then He rose from the grave three days later as prophesied, and was witnessed by Mary Magdalene at the tomb, and many others over the course of 40 days. Jesus Christ solely redeemed all things on earth. He redeemed earth time and catapulted us into eternal time. In this universal shift of time, now those who believe in Jesus have been catapulted into eternal time with all its eternal benefits in the here and now, in earth time. The curse of the fall of man has been redeemed by the shed blood of Jesus Christ, and now we are called as citizens of the Kingdom of Heaven to bring the revelation of Heaven and eternal time into earth time, as long as it is called *"today"* (Hebrews 3:13).

In this book, I share with you the importance of walking in the reality of eternal time on earth today. Eternal time is a time zone that all believers in Jesus Christ have access to because of His death, burial, resurrection, and ascension. In this eternal time zone, we have access to a realm with no beginning and no end, and the confines of earth time is sandwiched within the everlasting realm of eternal time. Jesus gave us access to the eternal time zone, and now we must learn to live in it—and from here bring Heaven to earth. Join me for the next 12 chapters as I reveal to you how we can make this happen.

When I have applied this revelation, I have seen personal mind shifts that have encouraged a greater knowledge of God's love and goodness, which has brought forth signs, miracles, and wonders. When the church grabs a hold of this revelation of eternal time and begins to work it out in earth time, we will experience the greater benefits of a life filled with rest, peace and joy of eternal realms. The toiling of our lives will cease, and we will we begin to till the land alongside the Holy Spirit, as we realize the blessings that belong to us as sons and daughters of the King. This revelation ignites our spiritual gifts for revival and reformation, as we carry out God's plans in earth time and bring the Kingdom of Heaven, its culture, and eternal time benefits to earth.

1 ETERNAL TIME

In October 2023, I took a trip around the world. I traveled from Jacksonville, Florida, in the USA to Athens, Greece, then to Doha, the capital of Qatar, then on to Brisbane, Australia. From Brisbane I returned to San Francisco in the US and back to Jacksonville—all within two weeks. I traveled around the world and stopped at many locations to minister. The first part of the journey from Jacksonville to Brisbane, Australia, I ministered in Queensland.

The first night I was there, I could not stop spinning in my sleep. It seemed I was in a supernatural time vortex. I had physically gone around the world through all the time zones on the earthly map. In this encounter or vortex of spinning in my dreams, I woke up and the Lord spoke to my heart that He was going to teach me about eternal time. I had passed through all the time zones, and I was returning home in a few days and I would have completed my world tour of time, and a portal of time was being opened up to me. I would now be given new understanding about time.

This book contains the greater revelations I received about cracking the time code of earthly restrictions and beginning to move into the realms of eternal time where there is no beginning and no end. Another revelation of time I received was the wisdom to know how Jesus's death, burial, and resurrection defeated time restrictions that originated from the curse of the fall of man. We can now walk in greater power and miracles when we know time has been redeemed and we are catapulted out of earth time and into eternal time simply by our faith in what Jesus did. This is the essence of being children of God given the power to crack the time code every day. He is the timeless One, and He entered a time restriction to release this restriction so we could now be timeless, just as He is.

Einstein's Theory of Relativity

Albert Einstein discovered the Theory of Relativity, which is all about the power of "frame of reference," a science that proves our faith.

This "frame of reference" is a subjective truth based on the lens of the viewer. The theory of relativity is defined as, "Different observers, depending on their speed, will disagree on what *now* is." Einstein thought that time might have been an illusion.

We can practice our frame of reference, as each one of us are our own observer in the "theory of relativity" or the "illusion of time." If in our field of view lies the future in earth time and we slow ourselves down to reach the future, then we gain control over our present as we are moving toward the future.

Part of our frustration in earth time is how fast we move and how fast our will pushes us to gain because of the fall of man. We must learn to have control over our natural sight and hearing by faith. Even Jesus taught us this in His miracle of resurrecting Lazarus from the dead. Jesus showed up after four days of

Lazarus being dead in the earth realms. He knew God was in charge of bringing eternal time into earth time and defeating the power of death. Although many thought that four days was too long for a resurrection from the dead, it was not enough to rush Jesus out of the will of God and God's timing by faith. Jesus had to believe God would raise Lazarus even if earth time said four days is too long (John 11:17). We are subject to what binds us. If our faith sets us free, in that Jesus redeemed all things, we are free now to advance by faith and to stop gaining or toiling from the curse of the fall. We have the power to defeat the time restrictions put on us by faith.

Eternal Time Is Now

I have some things to teach you about time. I know you've been working hard. You've been toiling, you've been moving quickly. You've been trying to beat the clock. What I am going to teach you in this book is going to help you crack the time code and step into the place of eternal living, a place of peace and rest, even while everywhere your foot treads, you will take the land.

When Jesus died, was buried, and then resurrected, He broke the power of sin and death in the grave. And when He ascended, He took the church with Him. I'm so excited about this reality because although I walk on earth, I'm seated with Him in heavenly places (Ephesians 2:6). When we know how to operate from the realms of the ascension or eternal realms, everything changes for us. Our lives become so much more fruitful, so much more prosperous, and we can lengthen our time. When you come to know Jesus as your Lord and Savior, you became "eternity in action." What that means is that as a believer your spirit and your soul immediately entered the realms of eternity, but your body, or earth suit, is here now on earth.

The Earth Zone

This type of "earth zone" living effects our body and is a way that God never intended for us to live. Do you know that in the Garden of Eden everything was beautiful, it was perfect, and God made everything delightful? It was fruitful and there was no death at all until the vile serpent came into the Garden and convinced Eve that she was somebody she was not. Eve was just like God. She was created in the image of God.

Genesis 1:26 (KJV) reads,

> And God said, Let us make man in our image, after our likeness: and let them have dominion over the fish of the sea, and over the fowl of the air, and over the cattle, and over all the earth, and over every creeping thing that creepeth upon the earth.

In this beautiful Garden of Eden, with everything supplied for them, and most important being in fellowship with God, this devious serpent told her if she ate from the tree of the knowledge of good and evil, she would be like God. God had warned Eve and Adam both that if they ate from the tree of the knowledge of good and evil, they would die. They clearly did not know what that really meant, but nonetheless, death would come upon them, and the enemy, satan, knew that. This enemy very much wanted Adam and Eve to eat from that tree because once they did, they would surely die.

> Now the serpent was more subtil than any beast of the field which the Lord God had made. And he said unto the woman, Yea, hath God said, Ye shall not eat of every tree of the garden? And the woman said unto the serpent, We may eat of the fruit of the trees of the garden:

> But of the fruit of the tree which is in the midst of the garden, God hath said, Ye shall not eat of it, neither shall ye touch it, lest ye die. And the serpent said unto the woman, Ye shall not surely die (Genesis 3:1-4 KJV).

What type of death is this anyway? This word *die* in the Hebrew is *muth;* it means to be a dead body, to destroy. It means now they would come to know eternal death in spirit, soul, and body. It means a permanent separation between humanity—between all of us who are descendants of Adam and Eve—and a relationship with Father God. They would be separated not only spiritually but also physically in that they would have to leave eternal time and enter a new time zone, called earth time. To die means that all remnants of eternal life would be removed from humankind and now they would be surrounded by death in spirit, soul, and body, and cast into a dominion of darkness of sin and death. This darkness meant that time would end.

Time was timeless, without beginning and end in the Garden of Eden when they walked with God—but now the scenario changes and death enters and time stops in the eternal. They now enter earth time, a limited time and dominion of space where they must fend for themselves in darkness with no eyesight of the spirit anymore or fellowship with the Father. This was eternal death and its effects on humanity and on our world today is devastating. This is a new time zone not originally planned by God; however, He knew we would fall. Today we are all born into this limited earth time zone, with its restrictions and lack and depravity. It is exactly *muth,* it is to destroy. All of us have been born into the earth time zone—a realm of death.

God had already planned in His great sovereignty to send Jesus to earth to save us—even before Adam and Eve sinned—to reconcile us back to God and to Garden of Eden living. This type of Garden of Eden living is what the ascension realms or eternal heavenly realms are all about. Let me help you get some terminology straight. Now ascension living or being seated with Christ in heavenly places, or the eternal time or everlasting time, are terms for all the same thing. Ascension living, is one of the same terms, and it means being with Jesus, seated in heavenly places, in an eternal time zone where there is no death.

Death Is Lack of Time

Now, I want to talk to you a little bit about what happened when Adam and Eve were convinced by the enemy that something was missing and broken in their lives. They were convinced by satan that when they ate fruit from the tree of the knowledge of good and evil, they would then receive something special, but all they received was death—just as God told them:

> And the Lord God commanded the man, saying, "Of every tree of the garden you may freely eat; but of the tree of the knowledge of good and evil you shall not eat, for in the day that you eat of it you shall surely die" (Genesis 2:16-17 NKJV).

This death robbed them of time because another word for death is "lack of time." Have you ever felt that you didn't have enough time. Feeling like you are running out of time. Have you experienced a feeling like, "I have to get this done because there's not enough time." Why? Because we are the descendants of Adam and Eve and were born into what's called the earth time zone or the time zone of death. It wasn't our fault.

Adam and Eve, when they chose to listen to the serpent instead of obeying the voice of the Lord, took us into what we call the earth time zone or the death time zone. We wouldn't even be having this conversation today if time wasn't a problem. Clearly, lack of time on earth is a form of death; it causes us to do many things that are out of the will of God.

If Adam and Eve hadn't eaten from the tree of the knowledge of good and evil, we would all be living in eternal time. The best definition of eternal time is limitless living or having no beginning and no end. How do we know that? Jesus came to give us eternal or everlasting life and give us the power to live out this eternal life on earth *now*—not when we die and our body goes into the earth and our spirit and soul go to Heaven. Jesus was born in the order of Melchizedek, which means He has no beginning and no end. This is what Hebrews 7:3 (KJV) tells us, *"Without father, without mother, without descent, having neither beginning of days, nor end of life; but made like unto the Son of God; abideth a priest continually."*

Jesus is limitless and He lives forever, and that's where we were originally supposed to be if sin had not entered the world. If we were technically born into the Garden of Eden before sin, we would have been born into a life everlasting from the moment of our natural birth. Sadly, that didn't happen. It didn't happen because Genesis chapter 3 tells us that Adam and Eve disobeyed God and ate from the tree of the knowledge of good and evil.

But here's the good news. When Adam and Eve were told to leave the Garden, God put a curse upon the land, which brought forth toiling, hard work—the opposite of what they had experienced in the Garden before they disobeyed. As they were exiting, God placed a flaming sword at the end of the Garden. That flaming sword represented Jesus Christ, our Lord and Savior. The way back into the Garden of Eden, the way back to eternal time is through the redemption that Jesus Christ gives us through His shed blood.

Genesis 3:22-24 (KJV) reads:

> And the Lord God said, Behold, the man is become as one of us, to know good and evil: and now, lest he put forth his hand, and take also of the tree of life, and eat, and live for ever: Therefore the Lord God sent him forth from the garden of Eden, to till the ground from whence he was taken. So he drove out the man; and he placed at the east of the garden of Eden Cherubims, and a flaming sword which turned every way, to keep the way of the tree of life.

Knowing this gives us the key back to eternal or everlasting time; it is through the "flaming sword." If we take of the "tree of life," who is Jesus, then humankind will live forever. When we come to know Jesus as our Lord and Savior, immediately we are repositioned back to the Garden of Eden and catapulted into living in the eternal time zone, a life everlasting. That's one of the blessings that Jesus gave us. He gave us life everlasting. Therefore, time shouldn't be an issue for us. But because of sin in humanity, we are born into a death time zone that robs us of everlasting life. We needed a Savior to return to us what was stolen by satan's deceit.

Time Has Been Redeemed

Every day in the natural death is a concern. Death is something that comes upon us. It's a realm we have been born into, and we must learn to defeat it. But praise God, through the shed blood of Jesus Christ, He overcame sin and death in the grave with

His resurrection. Then He took us to the ascension realms, the heavenly places, to be with Him now in this place of eternal, everlasting life. Sin and death and the grave have been overcome—and thanks be to God through Jesus Christ, the realm of death has been defeated.

What does this mean for us and our lives now? It means time is no longer an issue. Time is not what we think it is. We simply must change our mind to understand how time has been redeemed and we are no longer under the curse of death that robs us of time.

I'm getting excited because I'm getting ready to teach you truths that will dramatically shift how you deal with your daily life. You will stop running out of time. Stop being concerned about not having enough time or resources.

Death affects our resources for provision, protection, and acceptance. We live in death realms. But God is so good and He loves us so much; and because of what Jesus has done for us, we're now being repositioned to learn to live in the realms of the ascension, of life, of Heaven, and the everlasting and eternal zones.

I know you don't want the enemy stealing any more from you, especially since Jesus redeemed all things. In Ephesians 5, the apostle Paul tells us Jesus redeemed time:

> Wherefore he saith, Awake thou that sleepest, and arise from the dead, and Christ shall give thee light. See then that ye walk circumspectly, not as fools, but as wise, ***redeeming the time,*** because the days are evil. Wherefore be ye not unwise, but ***understanding what the will of the Lord is*** (Ephesians 5:14-17 KJV).

Why did Jesus redeem time? Because the days are evil. What's evil? *Evil* in this passage is the Hebrew word *poneros,* which means full of hurt, calamity, ill, vicious, malice and guilt. Sounds like death to me. We need to understand that Jesus walked the earth to bring us life, redeem life, and put it back into the earth realms. The earth realms are death realms; they breed guilt, sickness, fear, pride, all the effects of sin and depravity. We are strong-armed by the enemy into the death realms—until Jesus sets us free.

Evil is a living zone where everything is robbed, stolen from us. But God sent His Son Jesus to set us free from this realm of death and lack of time. When Jesus died on the Cross, was buried and resurrected, He redeemed all things for humanity, which means according to the Word of God, He placed us back in the Garden of Eden, a place full of life and eternity where no death was present. The Garden of Eden experience is like living in the realms of the ascension, also called the heavenly realms or the everlasting realms, or eternal time or the eternal zone.

Testimony of Death Defeated in South Carolina

I was ministering this teaching on eternal time in South Carolina at a conference, and one of the pastors who had suffered a stroke months before came into the church the morning I was preaching. As he entered the church, he said he began to feel around for a chair because he felt as though he was going to have another stroke. He sat down in the back, and as he heard the spoken word on eternal time and the power of an endless life ministered to him, he felt all the symptoms of the stroke go away. He was amazed and at the end of service he told me in private, as he was not ready to tell the church yet. The next day he opened the conference service sharing his testimony with the people—how the power of the word on living an endless life and living in eternal time had saved his life from another stroke.

This teaching on eternal time is powerful enough to take death off and out of your life in every way. You can practice this word daily to see your soul restored and the bondages of death and lack removed so you can experience the peace and joy God has for you. Once this lifestyle becomes part of your everyday living, you can share with others so God can deliver them too.

Time Redemption as a Lifestyle

The Garden of Eden—ascension realms, heavenly realms, everlasting or eternal realms—is a place of great abundance and prosperity where nothing is missing and nothing is broken. That means time is returned to us in its entirety.

Many times, when we think about redeeming the time, we think about redeeming one or two acts of time in which we felt robbed, in which we felt like the enemy came in and stole from us or harmed us, or we had great trauma. Under this belief system, we ask the Lord to redeem those moments in our life. However, what I'm talking about is much more than a moment of time redemption, it is a lifestyle of living. In this eternal realm we learn to shift ourselves entirely to a place that is completely prosperous, completely full all the time by faith in what Jesus has done by satisfying the requirement of death and now declaring eternal, everlasting life forever.

Technically, *Jesus's death, burial, and resurrection redeemed for us all things all the time,* not just specific things that the enemy stole from us. When the apostle Paul writes in Ephesians 5 about the redemption of time, Jesus *is* our time Redeemer. When we believe in Him, we are catapulted into eternal time. This is not just moving past that one bothersome memory that hurts, it is much more than that; it is truly living in a realm of peace and joy and a place of everlasting rest, peace, and joy where time and *all* things in life have been redeemed.

You must get your eyes and focus off the one thing that was difficult for you. You need to discern and your eyes must be open to realize that you live in a death realm and a realm of lack and things will always be less than and not enough with warring and fighting of the flesh. This is part of the curse of the fall—when Adam and Eve disobeyed God.

We live in a realm of death where things are cut off and cut short—existing in a time deficiency. When we say death, we are referring to an issue of time. If we live eternally, time is not an issue, and we have a remedy for all other lack issues in our life.

Since the Scripture tells us that Jesus redeemed all things, now time becomes eternal in our life. And because time is eternal, it means you're going to approach *everything differently.* It means you're going to stop rushing. It means you're going to stop being fearful of what you can or cannot accomplish in a certain amount of time. It means you're going to view things from the fact that there's plenty of time because you now live in the realms of the everlasting zone with full time redeemed, which means now you can take the time to carry out the tasks on earth without fear of running out of time.

This truth excites me—I pray it does so for you too. So because time is no longer an issue, we live forever and we no longer are under a curse of toiling, because toiling is a component of a lack of time. Part of the curse that happened to Adam and Eve when they had to leave the Garden is to leave everlasting time and go into the place of death and lack. When that happened to them, they entered toiling. Toiling means working hard to provide for themselves, drudgery to obtain what they need because they don't have enough of something. However, when

Jesus redeemed all things and brought us back to the Garden, suddenly all of that was brought forth. Now there's no more toiling—now we can enter a mindset of rest.

Genesis 3:17 (KJV) says, *"And unto Adam he said, Because thou hast hearkened unto the voice of thy wife, and hast eaten of the tree, of which I commanded thee, saying, Thou shalt not eat of it: cursed is the ground for thy sake; in sorrow shalt thou eat of it all the days of thy life."* We will talk more on *toiling* in the following chapters.

Time Is Abundant

Do you know that supernaturally you have way more time than you've ever imagined? You have to shift your mindset to the fact that you have a lifetime, not only a lifetime on the earth, but everlasting time. How can this be? Because if you know Jesus as your Lord and Savior, you will never die. This truth is very important. You become born again in your spirit where there is no lack—you have all your need and more.

It's just your soul that tells you there's a lack of time and resources in your life. Your soul tells you that there is lack of finances, there is a lack of love. There's a lack of provision, protection, acceptance. Our souls breathe that, but that's not who we are in our spirit. Your spirit is alive and very much in connection with what is happening in the everlasting realms. It's possible to shift yourself entirely by faith to walk in everlasting time and its benefits, just as the apostle Paul writes in Ephesians 2:4-7 (KJV):

> But God, who is rich in mercy, for his great love wherewith he loved us, even when we were dead in sins, hath quickened us together with Christ, (by grace ye are saved;) and hath raised us up together, and made us sit

> together in heavenly places in Christ Jesus: that in the ages to come he might shew the exceeding riches of his grace in his kindness toward us through Christ Jesus.

It's possible to position yourself to remain in the ascension realms, the heavenly realms—or also we call it eternal or everlasting time—and from this place of faith to defeat the effects of time. When Jesus redeemed all things, He positioned us with everything we need. So now we can live life in the reality that God makes everything beautiful in His time.

Ecclesiastes 3:11 (KJV) reads,

> He hath made everything beautiful in ***his time***: also he hath set the world in their heart, so that no man can find out the work that God maketh from the beginning to the end.

This word *time* is the Greek word *eth,* which means "continually," and is broken down to the Greek word *ad,* which means "duration, perpetuity, eternity or everlasting." That word *world* is the Greek word *olam,* which means "concealed, a vanishing point, out of mind." It means that because of the curse of the fall of man, God has made it so we can't grasp time as we should. We have the *world* in our hearts or soul and this removes our understanding of eternal time. We see things as always ending, which is a result of the curse of the fall. It is time to regain this loss by understanding we can have the *"beautiful in His time"* be made manifest today!

This Scripture is from the book of Ecclesiastes, written by King Solomon who had much wisdom. Yet, he wrote the book of Ecclesiastes because he had come to a point in his life when he had everything, but he says in essence, "You know what, Lord? I want more wisdom. I want to know more about who You are. I want to know more about who I am." Solomon asked all of this before Jesus was ever born. Solomon's desire for more wisdom meant that God would speak to him about eternal things. That's what I'm writing to you about today—eternal things.

I encourage you to shift your thinking into the eternal realms and learn to live there. Make that your daily prayer.

Two Time Zones

Living in the eternal realm means that no matter what happened to you in your past, no matter what God's getting ready to do in your future—your life can reflect an eternal peace and joy. Because God makes everything beautiful in His time, it means He has "stretched out" time to accommodate every movement in the earth zone.

There are two different time zones, two different realms—the everlasting zone and the earth zone. When you were born naturally into the earth zone with earth time, you were born into the realm of death—but when you accepted Jesus as your Lord and Savior, He took you out of the death realm and catapulted you to the everlasting realm. Now from this new everlasting realm is where you need to learn to live your life.

This is not just about just the redemption of one bad day, or one bad and traumatic moment in your life, or maybe there's multiple traumatic moments, multiple losses, and multiple worries. The good news now is that the effects of Jesus's death, burial, resurrection, and ascension have properly positioned you in these eternal realms. This is true whether you are consciously aware of it or not.

For us to live from this eternal or everlasting realm today and not just when we die, we have to change our thinking. We have to start praying and seeking God for an understanding of this everlasting life that we've been given, an everlasting life that has no beginning and no end.

What would it be like to rethink every movement of your life from a place of peace and rest? In other words, catch yourself when you're toiling, catch yourself when you're trying to beat the clock. Instead, you can crack the time code with the revelation of how Jesus has redeemed all time and all resources in your life and how anything touched by the curse of lack and depravity He has redeemed. Begin to trod at the pace of grace to do all that God has called you to do, my friend.

I want to see everyone on earth living like we are in the Garden of Eden, and Jesus's death, burial, and resurrection makes this possible for us because sin, death, and the grave have no more power over us. Can I hear you say, "Hallelujah! Praise the Lord. Sin, death, and the grave have no more power!" That means anything related to death. Remember, when we use the term *death,* we are referring to "time cut short." That's basically what it means.

God originally called us to live in a realm of everlasting where there was more than enough time—then sin came in and stole time. We must understand that God makes everything beautiful in His time, which is everlasting or eternal time. Isn't this interesting to talk about eternal time? It excites me so much because I know that what Jesus has done for us is so immensely powerful, and the church is living a far less realm than where we should be. We have accepted so many things on earth and in the world as being okay, even the fact that we should be robbed of time.

That devil is a liar. When you crack the time code, he can no longer rob you of time today or tomorrow or next week or next year. He cannot rob you of your resources. He cannot rob you of relationships, health, finances, etc. Jesus came to defeat the enemy so we can live in the fullness. When Jesus redeemed time, He positioned us in places of prosperity and fullness and wholeness.

If time is still an issue for us, that means that something is still broken. But the good news of Jesus Christ is that He redeemed *all* things and nothing is broken anymore, we must believe by faith that death has been conquered. Because death is conquered, time is released and we are now living in eternal time. We must grab hold of this truth by faith. In essence, the truth of living in the everlasting realm today is by faith and faith alone! Faith comes by hearing the Word of God (Romans 10:17).

There is an earth zone where you are born in the natural and then you die in the natural; but the minute you're born again in the spirit, at whatever point that is, you immediately enter everlasting time or ascension or heavenly time zones or realms. It's then when you need to be trained to live in the everlasting. Church friend, believer, it is time to accept everlasting time to be made manifest today in your life!

Faith Activation

Now I want to give you a strategy. I'm going to walk you through a supernatural reality. I have a personal testimony of how God showed me through prayer and solitude in a place of quiet with Him that I could step into levels of peace and prosperity in the heavenly realms, even when everything around me was chaotic and in lack.

This heavenly place by faith has no lack, so it was a place where I could sit with Him and allow Him to supernaturally remove any desires for moving forward quickly—and to slow down earth time by faith. This place in solitude and prayer enabled me to understand the power of an endless life, which I will share about in Chapter 3. As I practiced this in silence and solitude, I began daily to live by faith in these ascension places and realize the benefits in my soul. If you want more information on how to practice the discipline of solitude and go deeper in peace, consider getting a copy of my book *21 Days to Solitude of Soul* from my ministry (contact information in the back of this book).

Now, let's do a faith activation to help you move into this place by faith. I want you to think about something you love to do, okay? Picture yourself doing something that you love to do. Maybe it's shopping, maybe it's golfing, maybe it's being at the beach, whatever it is that brings you joy, think on this right now.

Then as you stand there in that place, right now, in the earth zone, take that moment, that landscape, that sunset, whatever that beautiful thing is, the beach, the mountains, the golf course, whatever it is, and then allow that scene to move away from you. As you stand in that place or slowly walk toward what you love, it is slowly moving away.

This means that you never really reach your goal of being on the beach, seeing the sunset, finishing the golf game, or climbing the mountains. The beautiful picture of life that you so enjoy remains unattainable. It's "out there," but you're simply just standing still or moving very, very slowly, while what you love is moving away from you. You see it moving away while you are walking toward it, so you never actually reach it. Now, what does this mean? This exercise helps us understand the principle of extended or everlasting time.

Part of the issue we have with time redemption is that we believe we must move quickly toward something to get it done or finished. We think we must quickly run to hike the mountains, sit on the beach, watch the sunset, whatever it is. We must quickly play all our golf games. But I ask you to pull back and slow down. Let your scene be out there and just calmly walk at a very slow pace while you never reach it. That is what everlasting time is all about.

There is no rush in what you're doing, not the good or the bad. Having this perspective immediately stretches time. There is no beginning and no end to your enjoyment of whatever you like, be it the beach, mountains, golf, sunset, whatever. Everything fits into the eternal or everlasting realm where time does not end. Now why is this important? If you can learn to adjust your mindset, will, and emotions (your soul) that were affected by the fall, you will eventually slow down into everlasting time.

Realizing everlasting time in the earth zone is understanding that eternal time is working from a mindset of what is already finished. It is moving from what is done already, and then we do it. It is complete already and then we complete it. The completion or finished point is everlasting time, the point that is moving which we live in is limited earth time. We are complete and now we move toward completion in faith. This is why we don't have to race to the end or goal, we are in eternal time already; we just don't operate like we are. The sting of death or lack of time has been defeated.

This faith exercise positions you in a place in your soul, where you see this beautiful thing, but you can't reach it because that "stretch of time" lets you know just how much time you really have. In our humanity our souls are triggered to believe that there's never enough.

It is a curse on our DNA from the fall. If you can see yourself from God's view, you will know that there's more than enough time and there's more than a lifetime, because there is no end in the natural—then you have stepped in by faith to the revelation of everlasting time. Train your senses to slow down time and you will live out of the Garden of Eden experience, which is where you are seated in heavenly places, ascension places, in eternal realms.

Why is this important? Why is slowly important? If you're racing around and in earth time, things will speed by so fast in this realm of lack of faith in time, that you will have no peace or rest. Rushing reveals you are not living in what is complete or redeemed already, you are still living like time is not redeemed and you are under the curse of the fall of man. This takes training of the spiritual senses.

In this exercise, gradually slow yourself down and then take small steps forward, knowing that you're never going to reach your goal. You might say, "Candice, that frustrates me. I'm goal-oriented."

I totally understand, I'm severely goal-oriented and task-focused myself, which is why God chose to teach me this. "If I don't get it done, then the whole world is going to explode," that's how I think in the natural or under the curse. Maybe you are under the same curse and must get it done to be happy.

What I finally grasped, and what you must grasp, is that this attitude is an effect of the curse of the fall. You will learn more on this as we journey together through this book. When you begin to live like what I'm sharing with you, then you are walking in a realm of faith for eternity. Every realm you're reading about in this book is a realm of faith. It is true that Jesus died, was buried and resurrected, and defeated sin, death, and the grave. However, if you don't activate what Jesus has done for you, you fall short of the power that He's given you—and can only be activated by faith. I'm going to pray that your faith will increase.

This is just one exercise, there are many more I could teach you, but the basics are grabbed by a faith in the truth of the Word of God. Regarding eternal or everlasting time, there's no beginning and no end. You're called by God to live in the power of an endless life, and with that endless life, you can now walk and live and breathe in this place of peace.

But you must train your soul enough in faith to believe this happened when Jesus sacrificed Himself to save you. If you keep looking down—like Eve looked down and saw the serpent—at everything you think you must do, you're going to get swallowed up. It's time to recover your sight and move in all Jesus has accomplished for you in the realms of eternal time.

Prayer of Faith

I'm going to pray for you right now for an increase of faith:

> *Father, I thank You for my friend who's reading this book. I thank You, Father, that You're properly positioning this person. I ask You, Lord, to remove every veil from their spiritual eyes and spiritual hearing, that they would step into a new level of wisdom and understanding. Lord, teach them how to crack the time code and live in the realms of the eternal. I'm calling forth a belief out of you right now, friend, that you would learn to live in the heavenly spaces where there is no beginning and no end, and time is no longer an issue. That you would live in what is complete while you are completing your tasks of life. Thank You, Lord, that because time is no longer an issue and all has been redeemed, then my friend has all the resources of provision, protection, and acceptance they need.*

Now, do you believe it?

> *Father, we thank You so much right now, my friend and I. We're asking for an increase of faith to believe that*

> *Jesus really redeemed all and that we're called to live at the new levels of everlasting life. Father, we praise You and we thank You right now as we step into this realm of faith.*

Come on, step in with me right now. Just close your eyes and step in.

> *Lord, I thank You as I step into these realms of faith, new wisdom, new understanding. This can be done through our knowledge and understanding of the death, burial, resurrection, and ascension of Jesus Christ. We're breaking the time constraints. We're going to learn to live at the pace of grace, and we're going to know that when we do, earth time will come into proper submission and move with everlasting life.*

Your faith can shift mountains. Your faith can properly position you to live in the realms of eternity. Your faith is limitless. Only you and unbelief limit what God has for you. We break those limits now in the name of Jesus. Get ready for the next chapter as we go deeper into a revelation of the Word so you can grasp the everlasting realms.

2

Seeing the Ascension Realms

I had this amazing encounter with the Lord around Passover 2024. He opened my eyes so that I could literally see Him and what He meant about breaking the curse of the fall and the bondage of lack over our lives. The Lord was revealing to me the power of the corporate mantle that He gave us through His shed blood.

In the dream I was at a party and everyone was drinking wine and laughing. This man, who I knew was an Angel of the Lord, offered me a glass of wine. His eyes sparkled and He was so happy. I remembered I had taken a Nazarite vow and as such, I personally did not drink wine. So I said, "No, I cannot drink the wine."

Then this man said, "I AM YOUR CREATOR and I would like you to drink the wine." Immediately I knew I was speaking with Jesus. I said, "Since You are my Creator, I will drink it." Then I took the large goblet filled with the wine and I drank some.

Then He said, "Drink it *all*." Then I realized I was at a Holy Ghost party and these people were here because they had access by the blood of Jesus and they were drinking the wine of the Holy Spirit. They were being filled with His Spirit. In order to be filled with His Spirit, they had to first receive Jesus as their Lord and Savior and realize He shed *all* His blood for our freedom and access to the realms of Heaven.

Then I woke from the dream and God said to me again, "Drink *all* of it." I immediately went to Matthew 26:26-28 (KJV) which reads:

> And as they were eating, Jesus took bread, and blessed it, and brake it, and gave it to the disciples, and said, Take, eat; this is my body. And he took the cup, and gave thanks, and gave it to them, saying, Drink ye all of it; for this is my blood of the new testament, which is shed for many for the remission of sins.

I repented for my lack mindset and began to enjoy what He had given me in the dream, with no guilt or fear. Now please do not take this dream out of context. This is not about whether you should drink wine or not. This is not about whether or not you have taken a Nazarite vow. This is about Jesus pouring out His blood, and His blood in the New Testament is representative of wine during Communion.

I immediately looked up the Greek meaning of this Scripture. That word *shed* in the Greek means to *pour out!* This means Jesus is not just bringing a trickle of His blood to save us, He is bringing us a deluge of His blood covering! We understand this Scripture through our soul (mind, will, and emotions) of lack, which is so much different from what Jesus intended for humanity. In His shed blood, He took us to a place of overflow and out of the bondage of Egypt.

This dream was to challenge my thinking and how I accept so much less than what God wants for me—He wants to bless me, and you, with so much more! We can only receive from God what we can "see" through the lens of our soul. If our lens or our small eyes devalue or makes less something that God sees as great, we will diminish that blessing and render it powerless!

This truth makes me want to repent for my small thinking about His blood and what it can do! It can set us free from sin, death, and the grave and be the power that ascends us into the realms of the heavenly places. Who is this God we serve? He is greater than we can imagine and can do the impossible! Let us surrender to His greatness and love for us and reevaluate our eyesight. Do we see small or big? I want to see God as big, overflowing, amazing, superabundance, and more than enough!

Remove the Restriction

In this chapter, I want to help get you into the place of seeing into the eternal realms, which is seeing into the realms of the ascension or the heavenly places. Remember from the last chapter, these terms are interchangeable and represent the same place—eternal realms, heavenly realms, ascension realms, everlasting realms. I want to help position you with right terminology so that you know how to shift your center, the center of who you are in your soul, and properly position yourself to live in the place where God has ordained for you. Yes, He ordained this for you because He sent His Son Jesus Christ to reconcile us to the Father—and with the Father all good things are available to us.

Maybe you've been dealing with some unfulfilled promises. Maybe you've been seeking God for your purpose. Or asking Him about your destiny. But there's a restriction on your spiritual eyes. There's a restriction on your lenses. It's difficult sometimes to see or perceive where God is taking us when we live in the bondage of the earth realms of death. The curse of the fall in our

DNA makes us feel like we are always in a world of no time, with lack and no resources available to us.

In this earth realm, we may feel as if our life is unfulfilled. Promises have not been kept. The enemy has us blinded that God is not for us! But the Lord wants to take us to the place where we live in an understanding of faith, in His goodness, and the truth that He desires to give us a life of peace, rest, and joy. Yes, God desires to give us a life of peace, rest, and joy. We live far less than what Jesus has properly positioned us to live in through His death, burial, resurrection, and ascension. Jesus defeated sin, death, and the grave, and then He ascended and took the church with Him. This is what the apostle Paul teaches us throughout the New Testament; the apostle Paul was trying to shift the church to understand that there are new realms in our earthly existence that can be accessed by faith.

This realm we have been catapulted to in Jesus is everlasting and eternal and it is part of Heaven, an ascension realm. Jesus has properly positioned His church to live from this eternal place. In Philippians 3:20-21 (NIV) we are told,

> But our citizenship is in heaven. And we eagerly await a Savior from there, the Lord Jesus Christ, who, by the power that enables him to bring everything under his control, will transform our lowly bodies so that they will be like his glorious body.

You're a citizen of Heaven! This word *citizen* in the King James Version means your "conversation" is in Heaven first. But the church needs to get to that place of shifting themselves into these ascension realms, the eternal realms where our conversation and citizenship is *now*. We live far less than what God intended for us.

Everlasting Reality

Now let's look at Numbers chapters 13 and 14. The Lord spoke to Moses and told the people, in essence, "Moses, I want you to send some spies over to the Promised land, and have them get some of the grapes there for you to see how great this land is. Then they will return and tell everybody how good I am." That's what God was saying.

Well, that's not exactly what happened. Twelve spies were sent into the Promised Land. They came back with the goods and saw it was a great and prosperous land flowing with milk and honey. But then they saw giants who were in the land and became fearful and scared. Let's read the scenario:

Numbers 13:2 (NIV) reads, "Send some men to explore the land of Canaan, which I am giving to the Israelites."

Now let's fast-forward and read Numbers 13:26-33 (NIV) reads:

> They came back to Moses and Aaron and the whole Israelite community at Kadesh in the Desert of Paran. There they reported to them and to the whole assembly and showed them the fruit of the land. They gave Moses this account: "We went into the land to which you sent us, and it does flow with milk and honey! Here is its fruit. But the people who live there are powerful, and the cities are fortified and very large. We even saw descendants of Anak there. The Amalekites live in the Negev; the Hittites, Jebusites and Amorites live in the hill country; and the Canaanites live near the sea and along the Jordan."
>
> Then Caleb silenced the people before Moses and said, "We should go up and take possession of the land, for we can certainly do it." But the men who had gone up with him said, "We can't attack those people;

> they are stronger than we are." And they spread among the Israelites a bad report about the land they had explored. They said, "The land we explored devours those living in it. All the people we saw there are of great size. We saw the Nephilim there (the descendants of Anak come from the Nephilim). We seemed like grasshoppers in our own eyes, and we looked the same to them."

Then we continue reading in Numbers 14:1-10 (NIV):

> That night all the members of the community raised their voices and wept aloud. All the Israelites grumbled against Moses and Aaron, and the whole assembly said to them, "If only we had died in Egypt! Or in this wilderness! Why is the Lord bringing us to this land only to let us fall by the sword? Our wives and children will be taken as plunder. Wouldn't it be better for us to go back to Egypt?" And they said to each other, "We should choose a leader and go back to Egypt."
>
> Then Moses and Aaron fell facedown in front of the whole Israelite assembly gathered there. Joshua son of Nun and Caleb son of Jephunneh, who were among those who had explored the land, tore their clothes and said to the entire Israelite assembly, "The land we passed through and explored is exceedingly good. If the Lord is pleased with us, he will lead us into that land, a land flowing with milk and honey, and will give it to us. Only do not rebel against the Lord. And do not be afraid of the people of the land, because we will devour them. Their protection is gone, but the Lord is with us. Do not be afraid of them."

> But the whole assembly talked about stoning them. Then the glory of the Lord appeared at the tent of meeting to all the Israelites.

Although the spies were in the land of milk and honey, the Promised Land, they focused their natural eyes on the negative. They saw something in the earth zone that they didn't think they could defeat. They returned to tell the whole group the bad report, which was the land is good but there were giants in the land. Suddenly, everyone gets a wrong viewpoint of God.

Now, you might say, "Candice, I've read Numbers chapters 13 and 14 and I didn't necessarily read it from the standpoint that people were hearing a bad report about God." Yes, they did. Why do I believe that? Because God says exactly in Numbers 13:2 (NIV), *"Send some men to explore the land of Canaan, which I am **giving** to the Israelites."* This is important. When God tells us He's going to give us something, it's because He wants to reveal something to us about who He is.

However, in this scenario, 10 of the 12 spies returned with a bad report, all except Joshua and Caleb, who had spiritual eyes to see something totally different. They didn't see the giants. They didn't see the lack. The 10 spies went to the Promised Land and saw only through their "own eyes." Mmm...what eyes are these? These are natural eyes bound to the curse of the fall.

However, Joshua and Caleb saw through the eyes of faith in God's goodness. They had "spiritual eyes" or everlasting eyes and their faith had defeated the enemy's stronghold over their eyes. When we talk about shifting to the realms of the ascension or the eternal realms, we must understand that this looks way different from what we deal with every day.

Many wake up in the morning, then battle traffic, there's tension in the family, the rent is due, and on and on. These are regular problems on earth, but guess what? They are not heavenly problems; they are not eternal, everlasting issues. This is something to consider. These are earth realm issues that when we see them differently, they don't have a negative effect on us as satan wants them to have on our lives.

The fact is, when we keep our "grasshopper" natural eyes on the negative instead of by faith in God's goodness and His character, we miss who God is, which effects our decision making. If we want to talk about learning to crack the time code or live in the realms of eternity, we must completely shift our spiritual sight and our hearing. We must move away from natural seeing and hearing and focus on our spiritual sight and hearing.

We find in Numbers 14 that God was put off. Let's say He was offended as it says God was "provoked" by those who did not believe in Him as the Giver or the good God. He says, paraphrased, "Listen, nobody's going to go over into the Promised Land now except Joshua and Caleb, because you don't understand who I am as your good God and Giver of good things."

Numbers 14:11 (KJV) reads, *"And the Lord said unto Moses, How long will this people provoke me? and how long will it be ere they believe me, for all the signs which I have shewed among them?"*

Then read on in Numbers 14:26-39 (NIV):

> The Lord said to Moses and Aaron: "How long will this wicked community grumble against me? I have heard the complaints of these grumbling Israelites. So tell them, 'As surely as I live, declares the Lord, I will do to you the very thing I heard you say: In this wilderness your bodies will fall—every one of you twenty years old or more who was counted in the census and who has grumbled against me. Not one of you will enter the

land I swore with uplifted hand to make your home, except Caleb son of Jephunneh and Joshua son of Nun. As for your children that you said would be taken as plunder, I will bring them in to enjoy the land you have rejected. But as for you, your bodies will fall in this wilderness. Your children will be shepherds here for forty years, suffering for your unfaithfulness, until the last of your bodies lies in the wilderness. For forty years—one year for each of the forty days you explored the land—you will suffer for your sins and know what it is like to have me against you.' I, the Lord, have spoken, and I will surely do these things to this whole wicked community, which has banded together against me. They will meet their end in this wilderness; here they will die."

So the men Moses had sent to explore the land, who returned and made the whole community grumble against him by spreading a bad report about it—these men who were responsible for spreading the bad report about the land were struck down and died of a plague before the Lord. Of the men who went to explore the land, only Joshua son of Nun and Caleb son of Jephunneh survived.

When Moses reported this to all the Israelites, they mourned bitterly.

Natural Eyes, Small Mindset

We can see from the Word that these 10 men were suffering from small eyes and a small mindset. They saw the giants with their natural eyes, through the curse of the fallen when Adam and Eve disobeyed God. These 10 became fearful as humans do. When we walk in fear, we are walking in another dimension of death.

Remember that death ultimately means "there is no time." The word *death* wouldn't even be relevant to us if time was not an issue. When we say something is dying, it means something is ending. That word *death* means there's an end.

Ultimately, the spies were afraid of dying. They were afraid of death. They were afraid that something was going to be too big for them to control. They refused to see God's greatness and His goodness and that He wanted to reveal part of Himself in giving them the Promised Land. Knowing God is good and loves us and will provide for us is the kind of mind shift we must have if we want to live in the realms of the ascension.

If we want to live in the heavenly places and in the eternal time zone, we must break every natural construct. And we must first start with our eyes and our ears. What is it that we believe? We see different when we believe different. If you have faith in God's goodness, if you believe He's good all the time, if you believe that you have been resurrected and the power of sin, death, and the grave is defeated and you have indeed ascended with Christ, if you believe these truths, then you are stepping into a new way of seeing or perceiving by the Spirit.

We are called to live in the realm of faith and no longer see things through the eyes of death like these men who saw themselves as grasshoppers. That means they perceived themselves through their own souls as still being under the curse. They viewed themselves as little and insignificant, as being run over, as being abused, as losing opportunity, as having lost and are full of lack.

Jesus Christ died, was buried and resurrected to redeem the curse that lives in our souls and change our eyesight that we may perceive life everlasting for today.

Your eyesight needs to change. You need to see like Joshua and Caleb. They were praised by God as ones who had a different spirit because they could see, perceive how God sees. If you want to learn to live in the realms of the ascension, the prosperous realms, the heavenly realms, you must have a mind shift, a soul shift. You must begin to see and hear completely different. You must live like the curse of death is broken and you can indeed *see* big and *see* as God sees.

To realize the everlasting reality of the ascension realms, the heavenly realms, the eternal realms, our mind within our soul needs to shift to the truth of redemption of all things. It is true that the apostle Paul tells us in the book of Romans in chapters 5, 6, 7, and 8 that we died with Christ, we are buried in Him, and we have been resurrected with Him to a brand-new life. Included with that brand-new life are new spiritual eyes and new spiritual ears. We just need to stop operating as blind and deaf people and get on board with what Heaven looks like. If you want more understanding on this power of being resurrected with Christ, my book *Soul Transformation: Your Personal Journey* goes into more depth about this important topic. *Soul Transformation* is a six-week Bible study book that walks you through Romans chapters 5, 6, 7, and 8.

Heavenly Things

Jesus knew the power of being born again in our spirit, to begin the journey of having our souls transformed from the effects of the curse of the fall. In the following dialogue with Pharisee Nicodemus, Jesus talks about this process:

> There was a man of the Pharisees named Nicodemus, a ruler of the Jews. This man came to Jesus by night and said to Him, "Rabbi, we know that You are a teacher come from God; for no one can do these signs that You do unless God is with him."

> Jesus answered and said to him, "Most assuredly, I say to you, unless one is born again, he cannot see the kingdom of God."
>
> Nicodemus said to Him, "How can a man be born when he is old? Can he enter a second time into his mother's womb and be born?"
>
> Jesus answered, "Most assuredly, I say to you, unless one is born of water and the Spirit, he cannot enter the kingdom of God. That which is born of the flesh is flesh, and that which is born of the Spirit is spirit. Do not marvel that I said to you, 'You must be born again.' The wind blows where it wishes, and you hear the sound of it, but cannot tell where it comes from and where it goes. So is everyone who is born of the Spirit."
>
> Nicodemus answered and said to Him, "How can these things be?"
>
> Jesus answered and said to him, "Are you the teacher of Israel, and do not know these things? Most assuredly, I say to you, We speak what We know and testify what We have seen, and you do not receive Our witness. If I have told you earthly things and you do not believe, how will you believe if I tell you heavenly things? No one has ascended to heaven but He who came down from heaven, that is, the Son of Man who is in heaven" (John 3:1-13 NKJV).

You might say, "Candice, I don't know what Heaven looks like. I've read that people die and they go to Heaven. Sometimes they come back to life and they write stories. They write their testimony about their experience. But how do I know what Heaven is like?" There are many Scriptures in the Word of God about Heaven. The culture of Heaven is without sin and tears.

No one's crying in Heaven. Every need is met in Heaven. There's no asking for what you need because it's all already provided for you. It is like the Garden of Eden.

I know myself because I have been caught up to Heaven multiple times, and I write all about that in my book *Releasing Heaven: Creating Supernatural Environments through Heavenly Encounters*. I've seen the vats of Heaven where the gold and the silver and the grain, wine, and oil exist, mentioned in Hosea chapter 2 and Joel chapter 2. I share this in my *Releasing Heaven* book. I've seen the goodness for myself. I've seen the royal banquet table and people experiencing the glory of the Lord, which emanates from everywhere.

When Jesus came to earth, He came from the everlasting realm and eternal time to earth time. He agreed to come into earth time to meet a specific need here and complete the requirements of the whole law in earth time, and then resurrect and stay around for about 40 days before He ascended to Heaven. He met all the requirements that we need spiritually to take the Promised Land God wants to give us.

Shift Your Thinking

Our job now is to shift our thinking so we can take the land God gave us. We are able to move into the realms of eternity and begin to operate from eternity on earth by faith. In Numbers 14:24 (NKJV), the Lord is speaking about Caleb and He says, *"But My servant Caleb, because he has a different spirit in him and has followed Me fully, I will bring into the land where he went, and his descendants shall inherit it."*

In other words, God was saying, "Joshua and Caleb didn't see like all of the other spies did. They saw things differently, and in their seeing differently through their eyes of faith and belief in My goodness and greatness, it gave them supernatural ability to possess that land." If you want to begin to live in the realms of the ascension, the eternal realms, the heavenly realms, you need to see it to possess it.

You might say, "Candice, I can't see it unless I die. Right?" No, that's not true. You can know things about it and believe in faith. Your faith has eyes, your faith has sight. When we step into a faith that has eyes to see, everything can change, because we are seeing as God sees. Hebrews 11:6 (NIV) reads, *"Without faith it is impossible to please God, because anyone who comes to him must believe that he exists and that he rewards those who earnestly seek him."*

When God sent the 12 spies to the Promised Land, 10 of them did not see as God saw the Promised Land. Only two, Joshua and Caleb, had eyes of faith to see the goodness God was offering the people. The 10 spies had grasshopper eyes, as told in Numbers 13:33. They saw from the realms of death, they saw themselves first, not what God was offering them. Read that again, *they saw themselves first*. They saw their fear, their weakness, their lack, their fragility, their sin, their depravity—but God was offering them new eyes to see Him and grab hold of His vision so they could possess the land.

These guys could not possess the land if all they could see was through their own natural lenses—and you and I can't either, that is why we must put on our eyes of faith to see the promises of God made manifest.

I know a couple in the Bible named Adam and Eve who ate the God-forbidden fruit and their eyes were opened to good and evil, and they saw their own nakedness (Genesis 3:7,10). This is what happened to the 10 spies, they saw their own nakedness or smallness and it was too overwhelming,

I am inviting you to shift your mindset right now. You need to stop seeing from your natural eyes first and say, "Lord, give me the faith to see it as You want to give it to me." You may need to write that down. Say, "Lord, I want to have eyes to see as You want to give to me." God was revealing to these spies that He had something to give them, but they were so concerned with their insufficiency that they were unable to take the land. Their faith was crippled.

Unfulfilled promises in your life, death surrounding you, losses, trauma, lack of anything will cripple your eyesight and you will become a grasshopper right where you are. You need to break that grasshopper mentality off of you right now, in the mighty name of Jesus. You need to rip off and toss away that lens of "I am a grasshopper and I have lack." Your need to properly position yourself to receive as God wants to give, which first and foremost is, "He wants to give me the land."

Now listen, God wants to give you the promises of the eternal realms. Why would He send His Son Jesus if He didn't plan on redeeming everything and putting us back in the Garden? Jesus conquered sin, death, and the grave—that is what we believe! We believe the Good News that He conquered sin, death, and the grave, and then He repositioned us to be seated with Him in the heavenly realms of ascension and eternal and everlasting life.

Everywhere You Tread in Earth Time

Because you believe in Jesus, technically according to the spiritual truths of God's Word, the Bible, you now have a new land where you dwell in by faith. Joshua 1:3 (KJV) reads, *"Every place that the sole of your foot shall tread upon, that have I given unto you, as I said unto Moses."*

Here in the book of Joshua, we read about Joshua the great warrior whom God gave the leadership reins to take the people into the Promised Land. Joshua does not see from his unfulfilled promises, his limited life, what his financial situation looks like or what his family looks like. That is not Joshua's view. He views from the heart of God, the Giver. In Joshua 1:3, God speaks to Joshua about some of his next steps to take the Promised Land.

Just like Joshua, you must see as God sees if you want the things that He wants to give, or you won't be able to manage what He's giving you. Otherwise, the enemy will rob you and keep you in that place of death, the effects of the realm of death, and you won't have enough strength to receive what God wants to give you or sustain it.

You have to stretch your limits by faith and join God and His limitless perspective. The word *foot* in Hebrew means "regel," to "possess time," and to bring one from death to life. When God says, "Listen, Joshua, I want to give you the Promised Land, and everywhere you walk, you're going to possess time," that means part of redemption from death is that eternal time was bought back to us as individuals.

God intends you to flourish in the land that He's given you, so you must have time redeemed. God says to Joshua, "By your faith, Joshua, everywhere your foot treads, I'm going to give you the land and you will now possess time." It means death will be defeated. Because remember I shared with you that another word for *death* equals "lack of time." As you tread along in your life on earth, your spirit and soul are living in the realms of the everlasting, which is heavenly or ascension realms just like in appearance and the feel of the Garden of Eden.

This means that you tread in earth time and you possess time back. This is straight up from the word of God. The Hebrew word says we will "possess time"; and if you can possess time, you can do anything. It means you can turn every lack around and all that God has promised you shall come to pass.

Do you want to know how to redeem those unfulfilled promises, how to bring back loss, and how to be healed from that trauma? The key is in understanding how God redeemed the time on earth back to eternal time, and how He has given us new eyes to see this by faith—and when we do, it will change everything.

You can keep focusing on yourself and your problem. You can keep focusing on the lies of the enemy that God isn't good enough and He doesn't want to give you anything—or you can focus on what God spoke through Moses to those spies, "Take that land, I want to give it to you." God wants to give you many amazing and beautiful and wonderful things, but you must start believing it. You must get out of satan's trap of negativity, out of the trap of fear, out of the trap of shame, depression, worry, anxiety. That is not the Kingdom of Heaven.

When Jesus came, He says in Matthew 4:17 (NKJV), *"Repent, for the kingdom of heaven is at hand."* And in Matthew 4:16 (KJV), Jesus speaks of the difficulty of humanity, *"The people which sat in darkness saw great light; and to them which sat in the region and shadow of death light is sprung up."*

We were in a kingdom of darkness. Once you come to know Jesus, you're translated to the Kingdom of light. *"The people which sat in darkness saw great light; and to them which sat in the region and the shadow of death light is sprung up."* Now, how is this relevant to time? Remember, time or lack of time equals death. These scriptures are referring to the fact that people, those of us born human into the earth are born into a place of lack and death. A place of no time, a place of unfulfilled promises, a place where the enemy is happy to tell us what we don't have, not what we have.

The enemy is always there to tell you what you don't have. And so here it says specifically in the Word that there were people who sat in darkness and they saw a great light. And then Jesus began to preach and He says, *"Repent, for the kingdom of heaven is at hand,"* which means it's made near *now*. That word *Heaven* in the Greek is the word *Ouranos,* and it means "the place of happiness, power, and eternity." Jesus is talking about eternity again.

What is Heaven? It's a place of eternity. What are we supposed to be doing? Bringing Heaven to earth, which means you're supposed to be bringing eternity to lay on top of the earth zone, which is the zone of death. Jesus arrives, and He says, "Repent," which means change your mind. It means in essence you are saying, "Father, I'm sorry. I didn't believe You, and I need to believe You, and I want to know about the Kingdom of Heaven."

Faith Activation

As a faith activation, I encourage you to ruminate on these words and ask God to "increase your faith." Say, "Lord, increase my faith for prosperity, increase my faith for no lack, increase my faith to live in heavenly realms." Repeat this over and over again in prayer; this is called "meditation," which means to ruminate on the Word, over and over again, so your mind can be transformed.

Meditation is not a New Age thing, it is a God thing. To flood our mind with truth will cause our souls to respond rightly to the Word. Joshua did this in Joshua 1:8 (KJV),

> This book of the law shall not depart out of thy mouth; but thou shalt ***meditate*** therein day and night, that thou mayest observe to do according to all that is written

> therein: for then thou shalt make thy way prosperous, and then thou shalt have good success.

That word *meditate* in the Hebrew is *hagah* it means to "murmur in pleasure or anger, to ponder, mutter, to roar." Wow, it even means "to roar." Let's roar in Scripture until we see the manifestation of all Jesus poured out His blood for, so that we would no longer live less than and under the curse of the fall.

"Lord, increase my faith! Lord, increase my faith! Lord, increase my faith!" He will do it, because He already made a way, He just needs you to ask.

You may be thinking, *I want to know about the Kingdom of Heaven. I've never seen Heaven.* You don't have to see Heaven with your natural eyes. You don't have to have a vision. You don't have to have a dream. You just must have the Word of God. When Jesus walked the earth and said, *"Repent, for the kingdom of heaven is at hand,"* those people hadn't seen Heaven except for seeing Jesus. He was Heaven walking on earth. Jesus has revealed Himself to you in the Word. He's revealed Himself in signs, miracles, and wonders. He's revealed Himself in history. All of this has physically been written and we read it in the Bible, God's Word. We can confidently say, "We see Heaven when we see Jesus."

What does the Word of God say about Heaven? Heaven is happiness, power, and eternity. Jesus came to break the bonds of earth's time zone and the realm of death, which means lack of time; Jesus came to give time back to us. He came to extend time, which is good news for you because He wants to give it to you. All you must do is receive it. Do you want to receive it today? Do you want to receive happiness, power, and eternal life?

Prayer of Faith

Let's come before the Lord and repent. I encourage you to pray,

> *Father, forgive me for I have sinned. I have fallen short. I have made mistakes. I have missed the mark, but I want to know You. I want all that You want to give me to be made manifest on earth. I thank You for Your Son, Jesus Christ, who died on the Cross and shed His blood and was resurrected. His sacrifice was to break death over my life, to break sin over my life, to break my lack of time and position me to dwell in eternity even today.*

I can feel the presence of God touching you right where you are. You may want to hold up your hands and say, "Father, I want to know this happiness, this power, and this eternity because You want to give it to me." This is an exciting day for you because once you ask God for forgiveness and you say, "Father, forgive me, for I have sinned, I want to know Jesus," guess what? *You are saved* according to Romans 10:9-10.

The Word says that anyone who confesses the name of the Lord Jesus Christ shall be saved. You have salvation. What does salvation mean for you? It means you now have a born-again spirit, and this born-again spirit is alive and will never die. You've already defeated death just by asking Jesus to be your Lord and Savior, and now you need to receive your spiritual eyesight.

"Father, I thank You that my reader friend is going to open his/her eyes of faith and begin to see happiness, power, and eternity being made manifest in the mighty name of Jesus." Through this prayer, God removes blinders from your eyes right now. I ask the angels to come and visit you in the mighty name of Jesus, to come to minister to you, and to take care of every need you think you have. It's already been taken care of in Heaven in eternal time and God is going to give it to you in earth time.

I prophesy to you today, "God is going to provide for your every need." Why? Because He loves you. Every need will be met because He did it through Jesus, and now it's going to come to you in the natural form on earth.

I'm excited for you today!

3

POWER OF AN ENDLESS LIFE

If you want to learn to crack the time code, then understanding the power of an endless life is necessary. You will never die if you know Jesus as your Lord and Savior. You have been transported to the eternal realms and into everlasting and eternal life once you come to know Him as Lord and Savior. If you have received Jesus as Lord and Savior, you have defeated the power of death over your own life so you can live today from the realms of everlasting life.

One of the main keys to cracking the time code is to know Jesus. Who is Jesus? He is the Son of God who came from Heaven to earth to die on the Cross for us, shed His blood, be buried and resurrected to redeem us out of the clutches of the enemy and the realms of death and darkness where time has been corrupted.

Our belief in Him has put us into heavenly places with all the benefits of everlasting life and eternal time. The time we lost in the fall has now been redeemed. This isn't just a salvation message. It's a Kingdom message. Not only have you been saved from yourself, but you've also been catapulted into new

Kingdom living in a time eternal time zone. This Kingdom living means that you need to learn how to live like you'll never die.

Sometimes people make radical and crazy decisions based on thinking they're going to die. Some people have a "bucket list," what they want to do before they die on earth. What if I told you that God has given you the power of an endless life through knowing Jesus Christ as your Lord and Savior—and you will never die. What you don't complete during your earthly existence, you will complete in eternity.

Right now, I can feel in the spirit that time constraints are ripped off you and you are starting to perceive in your spirit that you have time to do all that you want to do. When you know Jesus as your Lord and Savior, suddenly you are catapulted into a realm where you have more than enough time. You don't have to worry or try to speed ahead every day to get things done. You don't have to go at a superfast pace because, in essence, God has slowed down everything for you and made everything beautiful in His time. Remember, you are living from the eternal realms of completion by faith and now in the earth realm things are being completed. What is being finished daily in tasks in your life was finished already in the spirit eternal realm; you are just walking it out in the earth realm by faith.

Jesus Is the Timeless One

I want to share with you how the Lord did this, which is so amazing. Jesus is the Timeless One, who entered time and bought it back for us, so we could be timeless too. God sent His precious Son, Jesus, from eternal time into earth time into a set period, which we know is about 2,025 years ago. God sent Jesus from Heaven to earth to come into a span of time, live for 33 years, and do everything according to the written law of Moses. Jesus revealed to the people through His obedience that

He was truth in action; and not only was He teaching the truth, He was keeping the truth and He was in line with the law of Moses and with the prophets. All the law of Moses is summed up in loving God with all our heart, mind, soul, strength, and loving others. This is what Jesus says was the essence of the Ten Commandments:

> Master, which is the great commandment in the law? Jesus said unto him, Thou shalt love the Lord thy God with all thy heart, and with all thy soul, and with all thy mind. This is the first and great commandment. And the second is like unto it, Thou shalt love thy neighbour as thyself. On these two commandments hang all the law and the prophets (Matthew 22:36-40 KJV).

Jesus's mission was to come from Heaven to earth in a distinct period of earth time. As Messiah He met all the law, right down to earth dates, and earth times, and everything that was necessary. Then one day Jesus would shed His blood by being nailed to the Cross, our Passover Lamb being buried, then resurrected three days later, and then 40 days later return to Heaven and take His proper seat beside His Father.

Knowing and believing these facts is very important because we're currently trapped in a realm of death while living on earth. However, when we see that Jesus—who has an endless life with no beginning and no end—came into our earth-limited time zone and met all the requirements of what is limited, then transferred time and us in time to a place of limitless living. This truth is from Hebrews 7, where the author of Hebrews shares how we're called to live according to a *"new and living way"* (Hebrews 10:20); this is what Jesus was referring to.

I need you to stay with me as we look into the book of Hebrews as it reveals the importance of Jesus coming from eternity, meeting the requirements of eternity written in earth laws and times, so He can set us free of time restriction and return fullness of life to us.

Priest in the Order of Melchizedek

The author of Hebrews is speaking to the Jewish people about the validity of Jesus, or Yeshua, being Messiah. In Hebrews chapter 7, the author of Hebrews is explaining specifically what Jesus did when He died on the Cross, and how He broke the power of sin, death in the grave, and how all the law was actually met in a specific timeframe.

You might be asking, "Candice, why are you focusing so much on this specific timeframe on earth?" I'm focusing so much on a specific timeframe because you have to understand that when Jesus is talking to us about the Kingdom of Heaven, the Kingdom of God or ascension realms, prosperous realms, eternal realms, we have to know that He met every requirement according to the law on earth to catapult us into that place of the eternal, because in the fulfillment of the earthly law we are catapulted into eternal realms where our place of power resides.

> For it is evident that our Lord sprang out of Juda; of which tribe Moses spake nothing concerning priesthood. And it is yet far more evident: for that after the similitude of Melchisedec there ariseth another priest, who is made, not after the law of a carnal commandment, but after ***the power of an endless life***. For he testifieth, thou art a priest for ever after the order of Melchisedec (Hebrews 7:14-17 KJV).

You might be thinking, *Okay, Candice, that's great, but really what does that mean exactly?* This means that Jesus Himself is in the likeness of Melchizedek; however, many believe He *is* Melchizedek. Throughout the book of Hebrews, we find that Abraham meets Melchizedek with a tithe, and Melchizedek and Abraham take Communion together. There are set things that Jesus Himself identified as having an endless life, one that is indestructible. Acts of tithing and Communion confirm the validity on earth of what has existed in the heavenlies as valuable.

In Genesis 14:18-20 (KJV) we read:

> And Melchizedek king of Salem brought forth bread and wine: and he was the priest of the most high God. And he blessed him, and said, Blessed be Abram of the most high God, possessor of heaven and earth: And blessed be the most high God, which hath delivered thine enemies into thy hand. And he [Abraham] gave him tithes of all.

Before the law of the tithe was given by Moses, Melchizedek met Abraham and took Communion with him. In essence, Melchizedek, king of Salem, which means king of Shalom or peace, *and* King of Jerusalem was taking Communion and sealing grace before the tithe was ever given as part of the law of Moses. The relevancy is that grace supersedes even the law; and what God reveals in His grace through Abraham and Melchizedek is that Jesus—the King of Salem in the person of Melchizedek—fulfilled everything in having Communion with Abraham.

Grace is the key to enter into the realms of the eternal and to maintain and sustain in our endless life today. Life eternal was exercised in Communion with Melchizedek and Abraham early on in Genesis. The most high God is called, *"possessor of heaven and earth."* God has the power and through Jesus's death, burial, resurrection, and ascension, which is the essence of Communion, the eternal door of salvation and the conquering of the power of death has occurred.

Live an Endless Life

What this means for you and me today is that when Jesus came into earth time to fulfill the law, He came in through the endless life power. That power was enough to break the power of the earth realms, or sin and death in the grave. That's important for us because Jesus is in the order of an endless life and He says that the church is seated with Him in heavenly places; so, we're in this space with Him and are the recipients of an endless life too.

Knowing you have the power of an endless life can completely change the way you live your life every day. It'll change the way you make choices and decisions. It'll change the way you pray. It'll change the way you worship. It'll give you peace and rest daily in the restrictions of earth time, because the power of an endless life is the power to crack the time code of stress and overwork in today's world.

It is the power to live a redeemed life because time has been redeemed by the One who holds the power of an endless life. To redeem life defeats the power of death, as death just means that time is ending. This is why the time code is cracked by Jesus, our Passover Lamb.

Our Lord and Savior, Yeshua, Messiah, is in the order of Melchizedek. He is the one who came to the earth during a period, met all the Mosaic law and earth requirements, and then He resurrected and ascended, taking His proper heavenly seat, which now catapults the rest of us to living an endless life. This means we have the benefits of an endless life. Just like in Heaven. Heaven has no death. We are now back living in the Garden of Eden.

You might ask, "Candice, what are the benefits of an endless life?" That word *endless* in the Greek is *akatalutos* meaning "indissoluble." It means Jesus lives forever. Two Greek words together mean *alfah;* He lives a permanent life as in alpha and omega. *Katakluo* means "to demolish, to destroy, and to halt, to overthrow or thrown down." Through Jesus, life eternal is complete, which now destroys the work of the enemy and the curse of the fall of man in the dimensions of earth time.

Jesus was born "out of time," and then He came to "earth time," a piece of time to meet all the requirements of the earth time, to take us out of restrictions of earth time, and position us back into eternal time. Jesus destroyed the power of death. His endless life is more than living forever—it was destroying the power of evil, a dominion of *kratos* that I will speak of in later chapters.

You may be wondering, *That's great, that's wonderful, that's kind of theological and that's even scientific, but what does that have to do with me? And why should I care that He repositioned me in eternal time?* Because when you've been repositioned in eternal time, it means you have all the benefits of eternity now in earth time. It means that you're not limited by restrictions of earth time. You are not limited by what you see and touch. Limits on life come with time restrictions, but if time has been fully redeemed and we are now given eternal time benefits, then we have regained what was lost in the fall when the curse robbed us of time by bringing us into death. Death is eternal separation from God with the outcomes affecting the earth we live in and the natural states we are born into.

Access Your Power

An eternal endless life also means that you have access to all the benefits of Heaven, one of those being the riches of Heaven in the vats of Heaven. God is the Giver who wants to give you everything. It means that your conversation is in Heaven and that all the blessings that belong to you today first are heavenly and second earthly.

Jesus had His power because He had an endless life. So how do you get your power? You get your power by understanding that you will never die. You have an endless life and all the benefits that come with that—it's now time to enter peace, rest, and joy while you are still alive in earth time. All the benefits of eternity and eternal time are yours now in the earth time zone. This will stop every earth battle at its inception. All earthly battles are designed to draw you into a fight for your life, resources, position, etc., but an endless life trumps the earthly battle and removes its power.

If Jesus didn't accomplish all that He was sent to do, you could still have something to worry about. You could still have something to be anxious about. You might be anxious you are out of time and might miss your blessing or feel as though you don't have enough time to complete your assignment or task on earth. You may feel like you're in the 11th hour and just too late. You know what? There is no too late with God. He wasn't late in sending Jesus, and you are not late in receiving His blessing.

God is always on time. He's never late. He exacted the moment that Jesus would come to earth more than 2025 years ago to do what He did so that He could meet the requirements of the Jewish law and the prophets, so He could be called Yeshua Messiah. Then He could take His church to where we now live—in the power of never dying, which is the ultimate power over the enemy and his tactics; this is even the power to subdue your own flesh.

Testimony of Power of Endless Life

I was ministering this message in Denmark at a conference. I began to share on the power of an endless life and I offered a faith activation, like the one in Chapter 1. I asked the congregation to begin to see themselves in a very special place they loved and to fix their eyes on this place. Maybe they wanted to fix their eyes on a picture of Jesus. Whatever it was. Then I told them to slowly move toward the image they saw, and then imagine the place was moving away from them. They all did as I instructed.

One man was picturing a golf course and he was enjoying walking on this golf course. As he did this, he saw a hole on the course, but he could not reach the hole as he was moving slowly and it was going away from him. Immediately he felt the power of the Lord come over his body in the meeting and he felt fire on his body and his stomach started shrinking. He had been asking God to shrink his stomach as he was hoping to get in shape and lose some weight.

Immediately, God began to answer the man's prayer and he felt that the size of his stomach was decreasing. He stayed in this place a while and felt the fire of God. After the faith activation exercise, he said he felt rested and in a place where God had redeemed time and removed his urge to overeat. His wife mentioned she had an encounter too, that she was very goal-oriented, and after the faith activation that day, she felt the power to slow down time in her life. That she could get on eternal time and slow down the effects of earth time making her speed through life. She knew that the goals were met in eternity, and she could now slow down in earth time and rest while she was working. She was applying completion from the endless life or eternal realms to what seemed unfinished in the earth realms. She was putting what was finished and made perfect in the endless life to the earth time space of what needed to be done. Both people applied the truth that Jesus has put us inside eternal time first. That earth time is a product of eternal time, not the other way around. We don't race to gain time—we live out of what exists and what is coming, but it is all accomplished and made perfect already in eternal realms. So, I encourage you to rest as you go forward in life.

I have seen this in my own life in regard to ministry and finances. If I try and force something to work quickly in earth time, I only get stressed out; but if I rest from eternal time as if there is more than enough time and I have not been robbed of time, then I don't need to race, I can rest. I don't need to toil, I can do the work of the ministry that Jesus wants me to do with Him, at His pace of grace, and ultimately it is written in the scrolls and is done. I just need to enjoy it while I am doing it. By faith it will be finished in earth time, which is due time, in *kairos*—and earth time and eternal time will meet in a place of alignment and peace.

I pray these insights are helping you today. You should try this with a time of prayer and rest with God but also while you are working. Don't toil, just till and enjoy God and the benefits of the Garden of Eden while you are doing it.

Living in eternal time and not the pressures of earth time means that satan's limited in his ability to attack us when time limits are removed. Satan gets his power from the fact that humans have only limited time on this earth. However, satan was defeated by the death, burial, and resurrection of Jesus Christ, so he loses his power over time. When power over time is defeated, you can do anything you want for eternity. The benefit is that when you slow it down in the earth realms and enjoy the life God gave you, you will enjoy the blessings that God has stored up in Heaven for you today on earth. You will begin to pray differently. You'll no longer be so anxious about what you don't have in this moment, because guess what? You have a lifetime. It's coming.

Our fears revolve around not having enough time, exactly what the enemy planned to keep us fearful. Satan wanted to separate us from the love of God and His peace that was found in the Garden of Eden. He wants us to worry and be afraid. Fear only comes in when death is present and time has been cut short. The essence of death is that time is cut off. If there's no death, then we have eternal or forever or everlasting time.

Different Types of Time

But when Jesus comes in the power of an endless life, He breaks down everything that the enemy did to steal, kill, and destroy. Satan gets his power because we don't have any time, this is how death can rule and reign in our earthly world. But that's a lie, death does not rule and reign if you know Jesus. Death is only death from the fact your physical body goes in the earth as dust yet you live forever through your spirit and soul living in Heaven eternally with Jesus.

You don't have to wait until you physically die to pass through the zone of everlasting life. If you can slow things down, if you can start enjoying family, if you can start enjoying the things that God has given you, if you can realize that every day is a blessing given to you by God—you will receiving even more blessings from the Lord as you live in the power of an endless life. This power will overflow into everything you do every day.

The endless life power is heightened when we learn to be receivers. We are so programmed because of death to fear a loss of time and resources. Many of us routinely think if we don't get this moment, then it's gone. Well, technically, a *kairos* moment is when eternity and earth come into perfect union. There are a lot of kairos moments out there. Eternity never ends; earth time ends. So as saved people, we are to look at life from a lens of no beginning and no end. With this mindset, now earth time moves much slower than it seems within the continuum of eternal time.

Remember the "theory of relativity" is a "frame of reference subject to the viewer or experiencer." Therefore, if earth time is moving slowly at various points in time when it was written in the eternal, you will experience an earth moment occasionally.

Let me explain how this works and explain some more terms. First, from Hebrews 5:5-6 (KJV):

> So also Christ glorified not himself to be made an high priest; but he that said unto him, Thou art my Son, to day have I begotten thee. As he saith also in another place, Thou art a priest for ever after the order of Melchisedec.

This word *forever* is the word *aion,* an "age," also meaning "past, the world, a Messianic period present and future, eternal." So *aion* is in reference to eternal time or eternity.

Then we have *chronos* time, which is within an earth time reference: *"Then said Jesus unto them, Yet a little while am I with you, and then I go unto him that sent me"* (John 7:33 KJV). This word *while* is the word *chronos* in Greek; it actually means a "space of time or particular period." It appears about 53 times in the Bible and means "sequential" time; it is an earth time concept. But *aion* is an outside of time concept, a no beginning and no end eternal concept.

We can read this also in Galatians 4:4-5 (KJV),

> But when the fulness of the time was come, God sent forth his Son, made of a woman, made under the law, to redeem them that were under the law, that we might receive the adoption of sons.

This word *time* is the Greek word *chronos* and is even here in reference to fullness of time, which means there is a time of completion in earth time. There is a time when something will stop in earth time; we would also say this could be a *kairos* moment because it is a finished time point. Even though the Greek word *chronos* is used here in Galatians 4, it is referring to a sequence of time; but because it is next to the word *fullness,* it means *pleroma* or "completion." These two Greek words together is where time became full and stopped in earth time. I would call this equivalent to *kairos.*

And within eternal time is earth time, which is slowly within the limits of eternal time. A *kairos* moment is when a moment of earth time hits eternal time and something significant happens for your destiny and you know it in your spirit and soul (mind, will, and emotions). A *kairos* or "suddenly moment" is when eternal time matches exactly what's happening in earth time.

Born Into the Everlasting Realm

Kairos is when Heaven and earth hit at the same time. It's a coming together, in alignment of both Heaven or the eternal and earth or the earthly time zone. We talk about *kairos* a lot when we refer to what is being released from Heaven.

However, you had everything released to you before you stepped into it in earth time. This is what you need to remember: eternal time breathes at an entirely different rate, and it has way more blessings than we see happen in the earth realm. Don't wait for every kairos moment where eternal time and earth time sync in alignment. To fully enjoy the life God has given you through Jesus's death, burial, resurrection, and ascension, live out the power of an endless life. Which means you have no beginning and no end and live out fullness and completion from the eternal realms today and every day.

You were born in an everlasting realm, known by God, before your spirit, soul, and body ever came into the earth zone. You may think, *Candice, I was only born on one day and I'm going to die on one day.* True, but only in the earth zone. In the following Scripture verses, we have a similar conversation between Jesus and Nicodemus—cited in a different Bible version from the one previously offered in Chapter 2:

> Now there was a Pharisee, a man named Nicodemus who was a member of the Jewish ruling council. He came to Jesus at night and said, "Rabbi, we know that you are a teacher who has come from God. For no one could perform the signs you are doing if God were not with him."
>
> Jesus replied, "Very truly I tell you, no one can see the kingdom of God unless they are born again."
>
> "How can someone be born when they are old?" Nicodemus asked. "Surely they cannot enter a second time into their mother's womb to be born!"
>
> Jesus answered, "Very truly I tell you, no one can enter the kingdom of God unless they are born of water and the Spirit. Flesh gives birth to flesh, but the Spirit gives birth to spirit. You should not be surprised at my saying, 'You must be born again.' The wind blows wherever it pleases. You hear its sound, but you cannot tell where it comes from or where it is going. So it is with everyone born of the Spirit."

> "How can this be?" Nicodemus asked.
>
> "You are Israel's teacher," said Jesus, "and do you not understand these things? Very truly I tell you, we speak of what we know, and we testify to what we have seen, but still you people do not accept our testimony" (John 3:1-11 NIV).

John 3:12-17 (NIV) reads:

> I have spoken to you of earthly things and you do not believe; how then will you believe if I speak of heavenly things? No one has ever gone into heaven except the one who came from heaven—the Son of Man. Just as Moses lifted up the snake in the wilderness, so the Son of Man must be lifted up, that everyone who believes may have eternal life in him. For God so loved the world that he gave his one and only Son, that whoever believes in him shall not perish but have eternal life. For God did not send his Son into the world to condemn the world, but to save the world through him.

Jesus is challenging Nicodemus, the Pharisee who knows the law, saying in essence, "Nicodemus, how am I going to tell you even spiritual things?" Jesus is saying, and I am paraphrasing, "Nicodemus, what I am talking about is you do not go back into your mother's womb." Jesus is talking about being spiritually born. If you know Jesus as your Lord and Savior, you are born again, spiritually born, in your inner self, in your unregenerate self, your dead spirit, which now becomes regenerate or alive, and now officially you will never spiritually die; you will enter the eternal realms in that moment of receiving Jesus.

This is the most amazing thing because when you know Jesus, you never spiritually die. You get to live forever in your spirit and soul. Your body may return to dust in the earth time zone, but eternally *you* are in the eternal time zone and that is not when your body dies, it is *now,* at the moment of salvation. If you are living forever, your mind has to change and has to shift to who you are now.

New and Living Way

All believers have to rejoice in knowing that Jesus has made a way for us in the new eternal order of Melchizedek. There's a new order of life, friend, and it's called a *"new and living way."* I don't know about you, but I'm excited about this biblical truth.

My way is not called a new death way. It's not called, how can I manipulate death? How can I get around death? How can I prevent this happening or that happening? How can I live in a realm of fear? Nope, this is called the *New and Living Way,* which is really important because it only exists when we understand that we will never die.

This is the message the church needs to be receiving today. We're doing a lot of spiritual warfare, and we're fighting a lot of demons, but it's about time that we learn what the benefits are of the power of the endless life. What would happen if we simply had a faith level that measures the power of an endless life. We would defeat every enemy lying to us, robbing us, trying to do all kinds of crazy things to separate us from our heavenly Father.

When we eliminate the power of death, we eliminate the enemy's power over us because then we carry the power of the endless life.

> "This is the covenant I will make with them after that time, says the Lord. I will put my laws in their hearts, and I will write them on their minds." Then he adds: "Their

> sins and lawless acts I will remember no more." And where these have been forgiven, sacrifice for sin is no longer necessary. Therefore, brothers and sisters, since we have confidence to enter the Most Holy Place by the blood of Jesus, by a ***new and living way*** opened for us through the curtain, that is, his body, and since we have a great priest over the house of God, let us draw near to God with a sincere heart and with the full assurance that faith brings, having our hearts sprinkled to cleanse us from a guilty conscience and having our bodies washed with pure water. Let us hold unswervingly to the hope we profess, for he who promised is faithful. And let us consider how we may spur one another on toward love and good deeds (Hebrews 10:16-24 NIV).

I realize this is a little bit deep theologically, but understand that we go from glory to glory to glory. For example, the apostle Paul's writings are revelatory knowledge. When Paul started out writing the letters to the churches and as he's growing in his faith, and as he's being challenged for his faith, his faith is rising level by level. The church goes from glory to glory because the church goes from faith to faith. This is another aspect of stretching your faith to see vision that is much grander than a small, self-persevering viewpoint of what we can have. Or the me-focused mindset of, "How can I get my little blessing for myself?" Living in the realms of death, the earth zone, shrinks our capacity for living limitlessly.

Power of Death Defeated

The revelation that Jesus brings concerning the power of an endless life defeats the power of the enemy. Hebrews 2:14-15 (KJV) says,

> Forasmuch then as the children are partakers of flesh and blood, he also himself likewise took part of the same; that through death he might destroy him that ***had the power of death, that is, the devil***; and deliver them who ***through fear of death were all their lifetime subject to bondage***.

Who has the power of death? Satan. How is *bondage* described in the Word of God? Bondage is to have a fear of death—to fear that there's *not enough time*. From the time we're born in the natural through our mothers into the earth realms, we know that things are decaying around us because we're born into death realms. Fear becomes our neighbor and surrounds us. It's in our natural DNA, it's in the DNA of humanity that there's a time clock ticking and saying, "Your time is limited." It's like a voice that speaks to our subconscious saying, "Your time is limited. Your time is almost up." Therefore, we work super hard. Under bondage there's never going to be enough time. It's built into our human nature biological system. But praise God, through the Son Jesus Christ He became our Lord and Savior over death. He became our Lord and Savior over our lack of time that exists in our flesh and blood DNA of humanity.

Paraphrasing Hebrews 2:14, "Jesus has the power of an endless life, destroyed the devil who had the power of death." Jesus delivers everyone who has a fear of not having enough time, which is to have a fear of death. Hebrews 2:15 (NIV) says that Jesus set *"free those who all their lives were held in slavery by their fear of death."* Fearful of death, no time. "All their lives" meaning the time period of our lives on earth we are bound to the curse of the fall of man until Jesus redeemed time. But now we are free!

So how do we regain this time? Well, we don't personally regain it. We believe that it *has been* regained or redeemed through the shed blood of Jesus Christ. What does that mean for you and me? Time out, slow down, relax, love the Lord with all your heart, mind, soul, and strength. Love your family. Love your neighbors. Love your church, city, province, state, and nation. Go out and enjoy the world that God has given you.

I know this is a tough message because I'm telling you to go enjoy yourself when everything inside you is saying, "I can't do that. Candice, don't you know we're lacking this, we're lacking that...we can't possibly enjoy life. I must work too hard." I can hear people saying it now.

Jesus has not only made a way to stop the bondage through His death, burial, and resurrection on the Cross, but He's given you the power of an endless life. The power of an endless life means that not only are you *not* in deficit, it means that you are now in *abundance!*

There's a total difference between these two mindsets. It's not like you were only saved from death, you were also catapulted into the power of an endless life. Now who has the power? Not the devil. He doesn't have any power. *You* have all the power because you have power over death and will never die.

Can you get happy about that? Do you receive the revelation? I see those blinders coming off your eyes. I'm going to rejoice for you today. You need to share this book with somebody because they've been saying, "You know what? Jesus saved me, but I'm still in this mess." Believers need to know that they've been saved, but they've also been set free into a life that is endless and full of power.

This is such good truth! Jesus didn't die just to get back everything the devil stole, now we are going to get back even more—including a new way of living in the freedom, rest, and peace of Jesus. The church needs to get set up in the new eternal way, acknowledging that satan has lost all power.

Listen, we don't have just a little power—we have full power and satan has no power. We need to realize this and get wiser to the truth of how the bondage of death has been defeated and how it works daily in our lives, not just when we die and our body goes into the earth. Stop saying, "Candice, but you don't know what the devil has done to me." Listen, stop giving the devil credit. *Let's give Jesus all the credit* for the power of an endless life that is ours because of Him and His sacrifice. We get to align with that truth today in the mighty name of Jesus!

Prayer of Faith

To Defeat the Spirit of Death

I know some who may be reading this are understanding the power of death being defeated as far as time—but some may have a spirit of death looming around you. Right now in the name of Jesus I command every spirit of death to be bound in the name of Jesus. Every spirit of death bringing fear and causing emotional and physical harm, we bind you now in Jesus's name; and I release angelic hosts to come and minister life and peace to you and your soul now, in Jesus's name, amen.

To Break the Bondage of Time Restraints

Humans have a spirit of bondage regarding time restraints. We're going to break that bondage now in the name of Jesus.

> *Father, I praise You and I thank You that the spirit of bondage is broken over my friend who is reading this right now—that they no longer see themselves as having limited time, rather that they see themselves living in a realm of limitlessness. They live in this blessed realm*

> *because You have given them that power. They've been given the power of an endless life. Thank You, God, for making Your children blessed and highly favored.*

God has given you more blessings than you can imagine. He's *given* them to you freely because He loves you. You didn't earn them. You don't need to work for Him. Jesus paid the price to conquer death and He's blessing you. It's time to just thankfully receive what God is giving you. You will live forever and enjoy the benefits of everlasting life today. You have broken the time code because He is everlasting, no beginning and no end, and He is timeless and the Timeless One went to the Cross and bought back time for you!

4
Perfect Will of God

When we talk about eternal time and living in this realm, we cannot leave out the importance of the will of God made manifest in the scrolls of destiny in eternal time and how this impacts earth time and carrying out God's will on earth. Every issue you may be facing in life is covered under the grace of God, and His grace overflows from who He is—ultimately flowing into His perfect will for our lives. When we are faced with serious issues, we need answers to questions such as, "Did God write this difficult thing into my destiny? Why am I going through this? How do I overcome in this area?"

In this chapter, I help you discern three different types of God's will. When you grab hold of this revelation, I believe you will be catapulted into a new level of understanding on how much God loves you and that He has a perfect will for your life. This perfect will is a complete will! It is His finished will according to eternal time. He has destined you for greatness, just like He did Jesus. God's will for your life is written in the scrolls of destiny in eternal time. In these scrolls are the good and perfect thoughts of God for your life.

Jeremiah 29:11-13 (KJV) reads,

> For I know the thoughts that I think toward you, saith the Lord, thoughts of peace, and not of evil, to give you an expected end. Then shall ye call upon me, and ye shall go and pray unto me, and I will hearken unto you. And ye shall seek me, and find me, when ye shall search for me with all your heart.

To move forward in life, we must have the faith to believe that God thinks good thoughts toward us and that He did not withhold His most precious Son, Jesus Christ, to save us from the power of sin, death, and the grave and launch us into a new, powerful, and endless life.

I know sometimes when we're dealing with things in these earth realms and we're so full of loss and confusion here, we can begin to think, *Is my pain God's will for my life?* This is where I want to set the record straight. God's will for your life is for you to live in a place of peace, joy, and rest. A place of completion that is His perfect will. Jesus says in John 16:33 (NIV), *"I have told you these things, so that in me you may have peace. In this world you will have trouble. But take heart! I have overcome the world."*

Be Transformed in Your Mind

Jesus has overcome the world through His death on the Cross, burial, and resurrection, which defeated the dominion of sin, death, and the grave in your life. Because of His sacrifice, we know that God has a good plan, and His plan covers you with the blood of Jesus. He has written in the scrolls of destiny good things about you.

I think sometimes when we have difficulties, we begin to doubt and question, "Did God make this bad thing happen in my life? Did God want this destruction or these difficult things to come to me?" The answer is, "No." I want to speak to you from Scripture because no matter what I might tell you, you must have the Word of God bring wisdom and light to your eyes and to your ears so you can see and hear it for yourself.

Hebrews 11:1 (KJV) tells us, *"Now faith is the substance of things hoped for, the evidence of things not seen."*

For us to grab hold of the will of God for our life and believe it is a good, pleasing, and perfect will, we have to know and understand God's intentions toward us. God has very good intentions toward you. He loves you. He knew you before the foundation of the world. There's a whole story that's been written about you from an eternal and living perspective. It is time you grab hold of what that is and begin living from this eternal perspective.

This is what the apostle Paul calls God's perfect will. It's complete, it's full, it's limitless. The things that God has to say about you are good, they're holy, they're righteous, they're loving and acceptable thoughts. God sending His Son Jesus Christ to save us and redeem our lives is evidence of His love. God knew the earth would fall into sin, so He planned before that to write a story of redemption through Jesus that would carry us into His eternal plan. God's will is in His written Word and it's perfect and defeats world thinking and patterns.

In the book of Romans, the apostle Paul shares with us about the three different types of the will of God. In this book, he shares the revelation of what God has written in eternity about us and how this is taking place in this earth realm today. In Romans 12:2 (NKJV) he writes,

> And do not be conformed to this world, but be transformed by the renewing of your mind, that you may

> prove what is that ***good and acceptable and perfect will of God***.

The apostle Paul is encouraging us to not be conformed to this world and not live under the curse of the fall with death and its time restriction—but instead be transformed in our mind that because of Jesus's death, burial, and resurrection, the curse was broken and time has been redeemed. The apostle Paul's saying, "Listen, people, I know you have been through difficult times. You may be dealing with hunger, turmoil, financial lack, perhaps chaos in your family, and depravity in certain areas. But renew your mind by seeking God's will for your life—His good and acceptable and perfect will for you."

Conforming to the pattern of this world means to live under the curse of the fall and live a life under the stronghold of satan's lies, which is to live under worldly thinking and in bondage to worldly ways. The apostle Paul sympathizes with the people but says in essence, "Now is not the time to conform to this worldly thinking, held captive by satan's schemes and lies—Jesus redeemed your lack and you must live free."

Your freedom falls into three different types of the will of God revealed in Scripture. There is God's *good will,* His *acceptable will,* and His *perfect will* that is manifesting in the earth realm today. We are called to test and prove all three of these categories, according to Romans 12:2. Believe it or not, there are certain things happening in your life that are the *acceptable* will of God, and some are the *good* will of God. It is good to recognize each of these categories and how God has redeemed them all into His *perfect* will for your life.

Yes, there is a perfect will written in the eternal scrolls of destiny for your life and this perfect will includes the redemption of all the wrong done to you in every way. The written scroll declares prophetically the fulfillment of all these categories into the perfect will of God from an eternal perspective. When the enemy is telling us God wants bad things to happen to us, that we are not redeemable, and that we will remain in bondage, loss, and lack, those lies mess with our mindset. And we think, *Did God write this bad thing into my destiny and want this to happen to me?* No, God did not write that bad thing into anyone's life. That's why there are three different types of the will of God. That's why redemption is the key to the three categories of God's will.

God's Good, Acceptable, and Perfect Will

The good, pleasing, and perfect will of God that apostle Paul is referring too is what happens in the earth realms and are subject to earth time. He tells us not to be conformed to the pattern of the world and its lies of death and lack. Rather, we are to be transformed by the renewal of our minds to eternal-time redemption and all things being redeemed today.

So what is the good will of God? The **good** will of God is the lowest level of God's will, if we can categorize it from low to high. The good will of God is the Greek word *agathos* and it means that it is a "benefit," or broken down to the Greek word *kalos* it means "valuable or virtuous for appearance or use." It's a good thing, a benefit or good for a specific use.

God's good will from an earthly perspective was redeemed by the curse and is now eternally good. It could even be considered beautiful or even beautiful in its time. God makes all things beautiful in His time according to Ecclesiastes 3:11. This "in His time" is eternal time. It is the Hebrew word *eth,* which is broken down to *ad* and means "eternity or everlasting." You can walk in peace knowing whatever you are going through now, God will make beautiful in His time, it is good and will become redeemed and part of His perfect will.

God redeems the good and makes it suitable for His purpose. In retrospect, God's good will is a piece of His perfect eternal will because Jesus redeemed all the bad. We must agree based on Scripture that no matter what we are going through or have been through, God calls it good or suitable or beautiful in His time for His purposes. This is where the grace of God covers us in all things.

The second type of God's will is His **acceptable** will. This is the Greek word *euarestos,* which means "fully agreeable or well pleasing type of will." This involves our choices in life, so "acceptable" means you and God reason together. We make choices that God redeems, and we call this His well-pleasing or His acceptable will. It means that as you're going along in life and have choices and decisions to make, you can talk to God about what you're facing or you can just make choices without consulting God. Of course, it is always best to seek God's will because He sees from the past, present, and future, as He has no beginning and no end. He's writing your story and your choices into His perfect will for your life. He is writing redemption in your plan as you are journeying along each moment of every day.

Last, there's the **perfect** will of God, and that's the perfection of Jesus's sacrifice covering you and written in the scrolls of destiny about you. This will is God's perfect redemptive plan defined and put into the right place for great victory and the fulfillment of your assignment on earth. The perfect will of God is the eternal written will of God in the scrolls of destiny that includes everything that has happened to you or will happen that is redeemed.

The good and acceptable will of God include our mistakes, regrets, our ups and downs, the losses and the gains. The perfect will of God is all the redemption needed daily from what happens to us or what choices we make that are in or out of alignment with God's desires for us. This is an eternal word.

Parents Know

Think on it this way. If you are a parent, you dream of your baby's future, you think of all the good and amazing things that will happen to the child as the baby grows. You only have good thoughts toward your child and a hope and future. This is how God views us and how He writes in the scrolls of destiny about us. It is where God's good thoughts toward us are written.

But what we dream for our children sometimes does not always turn out looking as we imagined. Maybe the child's journey will be paved with great tears and sadness, or great joy and blessing, we don't know. But we can know for sure that it is perfect when God has redeemed all things within that child's life. We believe that Jesus's death, burial, resurrection, and ascension cover every lack, loss, choice, and decision our children make. We believe the grace of God is sufficient for every issue we face.

The same is true when the apostle Paul is explaining this to the church in the book of Romans. He is saying, "Listen, the earth is a difficult place, good and bad things will happen, there's loss and abundancy. You will pray through and reason with God about some issues and other things you don't talk to Him about—but no matter what, God has made it perfect." Wow! Can we thank God right now for His love and grace and thank Jesus for saying "Yes" in the scrolls of destiny to be our sacrifice?!

This word *perfect* in reference to "perfect will" is the Greek word *teleios* and means "complete as in applying to labor, growth, mental and moral character, as in a full-age person." *Teleios* is in reference to our growth in life into a complete and full man or woman of God knowing God and who He is! The word *perfect* in "the perfect will of God" means as we are going along in life we come to understand the redemptive nature of God in all things. How He loves us so much, as a great Father, that He sent Jesus to make us perfect, as in growth into fullness in Him when we submit by faith to the process in our lives. Wow, this is amazing.

God's perfect will includes our growth and moral character into the fullness of Christ. We are assuming our identity when we walk with God and we are faced with the challenges we have daily and we do not formulate an attitude in the earth zone of bitterness, resentment, guilt, fear, shame , effects of the curse of the fall, but instead we move toward knowing God's heart for us and His good plans of love and redemption for us.

Can you imagine life where every day, no matter what happened, you just knew it was okay because it is written into the perfect plan to transform you into the likeness of Christ? This plan is so good that no matter your losses, bondage, or lack, God will turn it for good (Romans 8:28). He will make a way for you to reason with Him through it so that all things could not only be redeemed eternally, as it is already, but you can feel and experience the freedom in earth time as you walk with God on the journey of redemption.

Yes, our Father is that good, and His Son made it so we could experience His goodness daily just like Adam and Eve did in the Garden of Eden. We can walk along in life without fear or guilt; but when we make mistakes or have troubles, because of Jesus we talk to God and He talks back and makes a way for us to commune until we get through the issue. Yes, this is yours because of what Jesus did.

Are you living this lifestyle of God's goodness? Or are you still under the curse in your soul (mind, will, and emotions), which opens the door for the enemy to lead you astray? It is your choice.

In John 4:31-34 (KJV) the Word says:

> In the mean while his disciples prayed him, saying, Master, eat. But he said unto them, I have meat to eat that ye know not of. Therefore said the disciples one to another, Hath any man brought him ought to eat? Jesus saith unto them, My meat is to do the will of him that sent me, and to finish his work.

The word *meat* in this Scripture passage is the Greek word *broma* and is broken down to the word *bibrosko,* meaning to eat, and broken down again to the root Greek word *bosko,* which means to pasture or graze to keep.

Basically, Jesus is saying, "I have My meat and it is the will of God, which is to graze in a pasture. This is to do the will of Him who sent Me." Grazing is a whole lot different from cutting into a steak and chopping at it furiously so you can get it in your mouth as if you will never eat again.

Rather, Jesus is saying, "I'm going to graze in My Father's pasture. That is My food, My will, to be with Him." If this is Jesus's will, it is His will for us too—that we would graze in His field. Jesus says we are His sheep who hear His voice, and He is the Shepherd (John 10:14, 27-28). In essence, Jesus was daily practicing soul-grazing or resting in the Garden of Eden pasture. He wants the same for us; we are His sheep and called to graze in His pasture of rest. We cannot be led astray if we hear the voice of our Shepherd and rest therein (Psalm 23:1).

God's Purpose for Good

Again, the good will of God means bad things can happen to good people, difficult things can happen that God will accept into the story of your life, and God in His infinite love and wisdom will redeem those moments and make them perfect in earth time. When we talk about the perfect will of God for eternity, these moments of the good and acceptable are ultimately written into His plan.

Romans 8:28 (NIV) tells us that *"we **know** in all things God works for the good of those who love him, who have been called according to his purpose."* The word *know* in the Hebrew is *eido,* which is a covenant word meaning "to see in the perfect only." The apostle Paul is saying all things in our life, the whole of those things, work together for good (which is the word *agathos* broken to *kalos* meaning "beautiful, valuable, and virtuous") to us who love God and are called according to His purpose. The word *purpose* is the Greek word *prothesis,* which means a "setting forth or proposed intention," and is broken down to *protithemai,* which means to "exhibit, propose, or determine." God's purpose is His proposed determined intention to do you good because He is good. This means everything in our lives that we touch or touches us, God will redeem and make right in every way in the eternal realms.

From Scripture we know that God works everything together. When difficulty happens or something traumatic that totally wrecks our life and our heart, God redeems that in the eternal plan and He writes it in the scrolls. That evil thing is now cause for our good and the good of others. Redemption is for us and for all those whose lives we touch—who can see our faith and our belief in Jesus as our Redeemer. Another phrase for God's perfect will is "God's perfect *fully redemptive* will." He indeed redeems life and makes it beautiful in His eternal time, and we can rest in this truth every day.

Now you might ask, "Candice, what difference does this make?" For some it makes a lot of difference because they believe God wants them to live in lack and bondage. Or they think He wants bad things to happen to them, which is the mind of the world and what satan tells them because of the curse. They need this teaching on the will of God.

Others know God causes everything for the good and they are not concerned at all. They see God through the eyes of faith and know that He's the good Father and that He loves them and sent Jesus to redeem all things.

However, there are many people who don't feel that way about God. They don't know that He's the good Father and that He loves them. They look at their life and they see less than in every way. They have come under intense trauma abuse. There are many things unreconciled in their mind and they think, *Did this happen to me because God wanted it to happen to me?* No, absolutely not. Evil is in the earth realm only and is the result of the fall of man and the curse that came with the fall. Evil is the result of demonic forces and the fact that we live in the realms of death.

God takes those traumas and redeems them and puts them into His perfect will. They are not His perfect intention but because of His goodness, He redeems them and makes them good eternally and beautiful in His time.

His perfect will is full redemption. He sent His Son, Jesus Christ, to redeem everything to make it perfect. You have to know that your setbacks have actually been written in so that God will make them perfect in the end.

Scrolls Written About Jesus

Because there's an earth time zone and an eternal time zone, we need to differentiate between the two when it comes to the will of God. In the eternal time zone, everything is perfect with no beginning and no end. That's what God is speaking about being His perfect will from eternity. Jesus reveals that scrolls have been written in Heaven about Him. The author of the book of Hebrews says that Jesus's destiny was written in scrolls. A perfect will for Jesus was written, likewise a perfect will has been written for us too, as His life is our example.

> Therefore, when Christ came into the world, he said: "Sacrifice and offering you did not desire, but a body you prepared for me; with burnt offerings and sin offerings you were not pleased. Then I said, 'Here I am—it is written about me in the scroll—I have come to do your will, my God.'" First he said, "Sacrifices and offerings, burnt offerings and sin offerings you did not desire, nor were you pleased with them"—though they were offered in accordance with the law. Then he said, "Here I am, I have come to do your will." He sets aside the first to establish the second. And by that will, we have been made holy through the sacrifice of the body of Jesus Christ once for all (Hebrews 10:5-10 NIV).

These scrolls are books written about Jesus. Notice that Jesus is talking about a destiny where He becomes a sacrifice. The perfect will of God for Jesus was that He would suffer and die on a Cross for us. This suffering was written into the plan for Jesus. This type of suffering was not written into the plan of anyone else. Now this doesn't mean we don't have suffering. We do, Jesus even says that in John 16:33 (KJV), *"These things I have spoken unto you, that in me ye might have peace. In the world ye shall have tribulation: but be of good cheer; I have overcome the world."*

The perfect will for Jesus's life was to save ours. Jesus's whole life was lived to save humanity from a curse that held it bondage to death. Jesus's sacrifice set us free. His death did not take away our pain or loss in life or the trauma we have experienced, as I said in an earlier paragraph; we will have tough times, but God redeems them all because of what Jesus did.

God has applied your hard times to Jesus's death, and Jesus overcame the world—and now you can overcome it too. In God's perfect will for your life is a story where you are a winner no matter what you consider to be a loss. God sees it as redeemed because of His Son's sacrifice. You can rest knowing Jesus took the brunt of everything so you can live a life of redemption, freedom, victory, and overcoming by faith in Him.

Our Days Are Written

King David spoke of how God sees our life:

Psalm 139:16 (NKJV) reads, "*Your eyes saw my substance, being yet unformed. And in Your book they all were written, the days fashioned for me, when as yet there were none of them.*"

And Psalm 139:13-18 (NIV) reads:

> For you created my inmost being; you knit me together in my mother's womb. I praise you because I am fearfully and wonderfully made; your works are wonderful, I know that full well. My frame was not hidden from you when I was made in the secret place, when I was woven together in the depths of the earth. Your eyes saw my unformed body; all the days ordained for me were written in your book before one of them came to be. How precious to me are your thoughts, God! How vast is the sum of them! Were I to count them, they would outnumber the grains of sand—when I awake, I am still with you.

These days written before anyone came to be had "redemption" as part of the story, which is why King David can say that. Jesus was in David's family lineage, but He had not even come to earth yet, and David was speaking of God's goodness and His thoughts and intentions toward David and that all would be well in the end. The end being everlasting or eternal time. When God wrote King David's days, He wrote good things to happen; and all things that were not in alignment with God's goodness and purpose in the earth realms would be redeemed.

We indeed struggle in our earth time zone, but in the eternal time zone, there is no struggle. No matter your difficulties, the enemy wants to hold you in bondage to the fact that all that is happening to you—be it good or bad—is because of you. The curse of the fall is to get us to focus on ourselves, which is death. The enemy likes to remind us when we didn't make a right decision, so we will live under regret. He wants us to stay in this place of bondage.

But! God has redeemed all things and He has a good, pleasing, and perfect eternal will today that conquers all the enemies' lies. We must keep our hearts open and keep seeking God who loves us so much that He sent His Son, Jesus, to redeem the world and our choices, to make us victorious in every way. Remember, eternity has no beginning and no end. Daily you are walking in an earth time zone that God is redeeming moment by moment and making a perfect will. We must continue to remember that we are going to live forever.

Now what's exciting here is that God's perfect will is eternal, which means when your body goes into the earth and your spirit and soul go to Heaven, there's more work for you to complete. There's a forever destiny fashioned in earth time and eternal time. There are more beautiful things that will happen as we continue in the work of the Lord in His glory in heavenly realms.

I'm so excited for you because I can see the veils falling off your eyes. I can see you recognizing the fact that just because something bad may have happened to you or you made a regretful decision, it doesn't mean it's outside the redemption of God. He redeems *all* things. In God's eternal plan, all things have been redeemed.

God's Calendar

I want to share one more concept of God's will in regard to eternal time and earth time. This is in reference to the Hebrew calendar. The Hebrew calendar is God's calendar based on God's time or eternal time made manifest in the earth realms. The Hebrew calendar is different from the earthly Gregorian calendar, which was established by the emperor Constantine and the Council of Nicaea back in AD 325. The Gregorian calendar is a worldly calendar and we are told by the apostle Paul not to conform to the pattern of this world (Romans 12:2). However, the Gentile Christian church has known the Gregorian calendar as its primary revelation of earth times and seasons and when to come to the Lord including Resurrection Sunday and Christmas day.

The real calendar according to the Bible is the Hebrew calendar and it was written according to God's call to man. God spoke to Moses in Exodus 12:1-2 (NKJV), *"Now the Lord spoke to Moses and Aaron in the land of Egypt, saying, 'This month shall be your beginning of months; it shall be the first month of the year to you.'"* This was the month of Nisan when we know that the Israelites left Egypt, and later in history, Jesus died, was buried, and resurrected as our Passover Lamb.

This month is usually in the March or April timeframe each year, but it fluctuates due to the fact that the Hebrew calendar is a lunar calendar, and the Gregorian calendar is a lunar-solar calendar. In the beginning of the book of Exodus, we hear God say, "These are My months of the year." Yet Constantine changed the Christian calendar to be a different set of times and seasons away from the Hebrew calendar due to antisemitism. We need to have a revelation of what is eternal and what is earthly, what is God and what is man.

God's calendar is His heart revealed to a group of people we know as the Jews or Israelites. Throughout history there are specific earth times when God called His people to meet with Him or come and connect with Him. These were written in eternity before they became manifest on earth. For instance, in Exodus 19 we know God called the people to come to Mount Sinai to receive the Torah or the Ten Commandments of God. We know He called them again in Acts 2, after Jesus's death, burial, resurrection, and ascension, as He sent the Holy Spirit in fire to them in the upper room. This appointed time happens to be the Feast of Shavuot or Pentecost, which is the second feast of God on the Hebrew calendar when God establishes covenant and gives identity to His people. There are other feasts and appointed times listed in the Word of God that are so relevant to understanding the times and seasons and being in God's perfect will on earth.

I mention this because these times and seasons are eternal and first set by God, but then made manifest in *kairos* time when we participate with God in keeping them. I share more on this revelation of time in my book, *365 Prophetic Revelations from the Hebrew Calendar.* When we line up with the Hebrew calendar, we understand the correct earth times and seasons and can join God in His earthly work. We can bring Heaven to earth.

Praise God, He redeems all things, even edicts written by leaders who did not do right. God is merciful and His mercy endures forever. Even if we have only known the Christian calendar and never heard of the Hebrew calendar, God works with us right where we are and redeems all things so we can go forward and be victorious.

Faith Activation

Right now let's take some time to reset our hearts after all we learned about God's will and timing. It is time to focus on decisions we have made that are earthly. Maybe you're feeling a weight on you to confess shame concerning a choice or poor decision in your life. Maybe you need to confess carrying shame over being harmed or doing something you regret—there are lies surrounding your mind about God. Maybe your difficulties have been so great and you've wondered whether they were written in God's will for your life. Maybe you somehow believed a lie that God was holding you responsible for every choice and there was no way He would forgive you or redeem all that has happened to you in earth time.

Do not believe that lie! God takes all your life's decisions and causes each one to be turned for your benefit, for your good. He provides redemption for you and for your family and for your relationships. One day you will be ruling and reigning with Him in the eternal, and you will be living out the absolute perfect eternal will of God. So let us pray and confess today, "Lord, no more of these lies in my thoughts about You and whether or not You love me or have written a good story concerning me. No more believing lies! I believe that You have written a beautiful eternal story of redemption, peace, and joy for me!"

These are all real concerns in the earth zone, but they're not in the eternal zone. I just want to speak that over your life right now. So come out of that hole of depression, fear, and anxiety. Come out of it now in the mighty name of Jesus and see the hope of the future. Know that God, in His good, acceptable, and perfect will has written an exceptional eternal story about your life.

I feel that in your spirit right now you may be struggling with your future, wondering if the decision you've made is going to completely mess up what's ahead. The answer to that is, "No, it's not going to mess up your future. It's not going to mess up what's coming, because God's message to you is good, it's pure, it's holy, it's righteous, with only good things for you!"

For our faith activation, let's shift our soul, mind, will, and emotions into the heavenly and eternal places, to where Jesus has given us access. I encourage you to sit quietly with the Lord in that place of meditation. The psalmist says, *"But his delight is in the law of the Lord, and in His law he meditates day and night"* (Psalm 1:2 NKJV).

From here in this quiet place, you are now positioned in the realms of the ascension and eternal, everlasting life. No matter what choices and decisions you make, if you are seeking God, your story is good; and whatever choices and decisions you make, God will cause it for the good. He's going to bring you out of every circumstance. He wants you to have joy and peace on earth.

There are two things we need to address in this faith activation. One is your regrets and losses and the second is how you make decisions. So whichever mindset you have at this time, the following are two activations for you to consider.

First Activation

Be aware that the enemy wants you to toil over your misfortune. He wants you to toil over poor decisions. He wants you to live in a place of regret. I stand with you right now in the name of Jesus, and we bind every spirit of regret upon your life. If you need more help in this area, get a copy of my book *21 Days to Solitude of Soul;* it will help you learn three postures of faith to take you to the next levels of silence and solitude with the Lord so you can reach the heights of Heaven we are talking about and defeat earth time and enter eternal time.

Second Activation

Maybe you need to make some choices and are seeking God for answers. We must make decisions from a place of abundancy where all perfection exists already. As you seek God for answers, do this with a mindset of completion. Do this knowing that you are living from an eternal realm by faith that is perfect and complete. This place represents the fullness of Christ and is where the perfect will of God exists. As you seek God from this heavenly place, remember that in the written scrolls of destiny for your life is a good and perfect complete plan. It is in the eternal realms where your future lies. You must call the future into the present. You do this by knowing that all is complete and good and now by faith you are going to walk out the completeness on earth. You can slow down and trust God because the moment is complete and done already.

Everywhere He is going to send you and everywhere you are seeking Him for is already complete. All you have to do is be sent from the place completion. The work that you are seeking God about doing has already been done and is final in the eternal realms. So bring eternal time into earth time by faith, and rest in your future being perfect. God will carry out that perfection in earth time. He has the power to do this when you remember that you have an endless life. The understanding of an endless life is faith-based understanding. It is revelation from the Word of God.

Because there is an element of faith here, stop fearing decisions and start trusting God that the story is perfect and you will carry out that perfection by faith in earth time. You must believe it is already done in the spiritual so you can rest and not fear, and your decision will now manifest in the natural in the covering of God's will. It is already done in the eternal and will manifest now in the earthly and it will be good. This is the power that defeats sin, death, and the grave. It is the power of an endless life.

Prayer of Faith

If that's you right now, I encourage you to say,

> *Lord, I need You right now. I need You to touch my heart. I need You to increase my faith so I would believe that what is written about me is perfect and it's beautiful and it's complete and it's whole. Even though I'm going through this right now, You're taking all the pain and causing it for my eternal good. You're causing me now to begin to make right choices and decisions by teaching me, by disciplining me, by chastising me, by properly putting me in the hands of the right people so I may grow and be like You. You are inviting me to an endless life of believing Your will is perfect and You make perfection manifest in whatever capacity that is. You are asking me simply to believe that eternal time perfection overrules earthly perfection, and now I can make decisions with freedom of choice and peace and rest and know I am covered under the blood of Jesus.*

All we have to do is submit to the Lord, resist the devil and he will flee from us. These are normal things that we go through, but the enemy wants to cast doubt and wants to hold you in bondage. The enemy wants you to believe that all things are not redeemed and you are still under the curse of the fall of man, but that is a lie. Jesus met all the requirements of the law with His blood so that the portal of time is open and we have everlasting life and its benefits today.

Right now, this is a moment of confession and forgiveness. Confess your anxiety and your fear over the future and say,

> *Lord, I know You have a good future for me. You have a good plan. It was written. Lord, I want to live that plan out in the earth realm and then for eternity in the eternal realms.*

Right now, I am going to dispatch angels to you to help you carry out the perfect will, which is the redeemed will of God that was written about you.

I want to pray for you right now that your mind will be shifted into this realm of eternity where death doesn't exist, so you can believe in your heart good things written about you. I want you to turn your back to the voices of negativity and evil that are trying to hold you in this one moment that you've been bound to.

I want to pray for those who have endured intense spiritual warfare. Perhaps you have felt "less than," you feel rejected, abandoned, or feel you have been harmed physically, mentally, or emotionally. I pray in the mighty name of Jesus that Jesus died, was buried, and resurrected to redeem you from every less-than moment in your life. Remember that the fullness of redemption includes *all* things, and He's catapulting you now into His perfect will that is written in the eternal realms.

If you submit yourself to the love of God and to His goodness, He will reveal to you the great things that have been written in Heaven about you. Jesus agreed to come into earth time from everlasting time to meet a law and a requirement that allows us to live in these realms of eternity where there is nothing but peace, joy, and righteousness. This is your portion. It is time to get up and start rejoicing. I can feel that in the spirit right now.

Stand up and start rejoicing, saying, "Hallelujah. Glory to the Lord. My yesterday is not my tomorrow. No, it's not. My moment of difficulty now does not dictate what's happening in the future."

You are now cracking the time code and entering into the realms of eternity, where nothing is missing and broken, and all things are made beautiful in His time. May the glory touch you where you are. May angels come and increase you, and may every blinder come off your eyes and ears to position you exactly where God wants you to be—to be your best self.

5

Enduring in the Kingdom by Faith

On October 12, 2024, I had the privilege of participating in a life-changing event for our world. This day was Yom Kippur, or the Day of Atonement, according to the Hebrew calendar. Yom Kippur is the holiest day of the year to the Jewish people and also to Christians who believe that Jesus died, was buried, resurrected, and ascended, taking His blood up into the Holy of Holies and placing it on the mercy seat of the Ark of the Covenant in the heavenly tabernacle for forgiveness of their sins.

Yom Kippur in Israel is celebrated with praying and fasting all day as the Jews wait to be forgiven of their sins, but they have no temple to offer blood sacrifices for their sin because it was destroyed. For Christians, this is the day we remember Yeshua Messiah as the One who is our High Priest in the Order of Melchizedek. He Himself went up into the Holy of Holies in the heavenly tabernacle and put His blood on the Mercy Seat. He said, "It is finished."

On this day in the United States, there was a national event that I had been preparing for a year and half, along with many others from Lou Engle Ministries and Jenny Donnelly's Her Voice

Movement. We had been calling for one million women—referred to in this movement as Esther's and Mordecai's—to gather at the Washington Mall in Washington, DC, as a solemn assembly to fast, pray, and take Communion together to declare and decree the shed blood of Jesus Christ over our United States of America.

Prior to this day, I had been traveling across the country and around the world sharing about standing strong to return God to the fabric of our nation, along with protecting children and fighting for our rights as Christian Americans. I also encouraged other nations to do the same—that God was calling His Kingdom to arise and take back the land by repenting and living holy and righteous lives, and also by voting biblically in their countries' next election.

The USA's national election would be on Tuesday, November 5, 2024. Up until October 12, 2024, we prepared our hearts with praying and fasting and seeking God to make a change. On this special day, we joined together. They say about 350,000 people came to the Washington Mall in Washington, DC, and 10 million watched online. This day was called of God and was pivotal in changing the course of history. It was a time designated by God according to His Hebrew calendar as holy. On this day, Yom Kippur, we stood in the gap for our nation.

Already Finished

A few weeks before the event, I felt great peace in my heart like the day was already finished and had accomplished God's purposes, yet there were weeks still before the actual day. I was going to the event not because I was asked to speak, because at this point I was not asked to speak, but because I believed in the cause. About 12 hours before the event, I went to a meeting with some who would be speaking at the event. I was invited because of the work I had done in media to help advertise and wrangle together the many who would attend that day. No one knew how many would attend, some of us thought maybe 100,000 or less. Anyhow, after the meeting ended, one of the leaders, Laura Allred, who is now the head of the 1 Million Women organization, told me that Lou Engle wanted to speak with me.

Laura called me into the back room and said that Lou had been praying and fasting for days in solitude during this time. Nevertheless, I was ushered to where he was and Lou said, "Candice, God says you have something to say, but I don't know what. Can you tell me what is on your heart?" I told him that God spoke to me about the importance of receiving an offering for the Feast of Tabernacles or Sukkot, which happens five days after Yom Kippur, according to Deuteronomy 16:16-17 (NIV) which reads:

> Three times a year all your men must appear before the Lord your God at the place he will choose: at the Festival of Unleavened Bread, the Festival of Weeks and the Festival of Tabernacles. No one should appear before the Lord empty-handed: Each of you must bring a gift in proportion to the way the Lord your God has blessed you.

Lou said, "That's it. You speak right before the offering." I walked away from that encounter thinking, *What? I'm speaking at the Washington Mall? You're kidding me. Lord, I've never spoken to this many people in my life.* I had seen in visions and dreams of speaking at stadium events, but I had packed away this prophetic vision of the future. But now was the time. The whole experience had been weird, as I never pushed or asked to speak, I only enjoyed being part of the group and giving what

God told me to give, which was access to my contacts and help to advance the cause in media and get the word out.

God knew He had ordained this time before my birth and had written it into eternal time. I was in peace and enjoying God. I was not asking or pushing, and 12 hours before the event I was asked to participate this way. The future was being called into the earthly present in my life and it was being done without my making it happen. This to me was the working of a miracle. It was written in my scrolls of destiny and now it was coming to pass.

Another revelation of the truth of the future being called into the present is when I heard Lou say right before the event—in reference to all the hours and months we had all spent preparing—he said, "It feels like it is done." And the day had not happened yet. In other words, the outcome had been written before the event took place. I had felt the same way during the days leading up to the event.

God Determines the Outcome

Now the end of the story goes like this, we fasted, prayed, took Communion, and smashed the altar of Ishtar, the evil principality of sexual immortality and her demonic influence over our nation in regard to sexual sin and allowing all evil agendas. Three weeks later, President Trump was elected into office. Since his time as president, he has done more to turn back the evil agenda of the force of Ishtar and sexual immorality than any president prior to him. He declared, "There are only two genders—male and female."

The reason for my story is that before we ever had the one million Esther-Mordecai event on the Washington Mall, the outcome was complete and the unity of the believers in communion and standing in prayer and fasting broke the curse of the demonic goddess of Ishtar in our nation. The power of this overthrow happened first in eternal time. This act has now carried over to other nations as they stand for righteousness and holiness and purity in their nations. We have much work to do but we must know that when it comes to prophecy, God will show us where to go, we must follow and He makes the outcome.

Before we ever set foot to move ahead with Him. He goes before us and He paves the way. We must have the faith to believe. We don't have to push and press, we just must believe and together be unified. This revelation was true for me personally when I never pushed to speak and it happened, and it was true for our nation when we believed God called us and we went to the Washington Mall. Our going was not in vain, it was settled before the foundation of the world—we were just walking it out in obedience.

No matter where you are in your desires and hopes for the future, no matter the prophetic words spoken over your life, the miraculous is made evident when we obey, as "obedience is better than sacrifice." God makes the way as we live by faith and He sets the future prophetic word into the present when we only believe. You can rest in the fact that the end is written before the beginning, and He makes the outcomes.

One day God said to me, "Candice, everywhere I send you the work is already done." Wow, that statement gave me such peace. I don't have to make it happen. I just do what He says. I obey and He does the rest. Now you think of some things God has spoken over your life and trust Him for the outcome. Know that He is faithful and will bring them to pass in due time. All you must do is have faith and believe and obey. He determines the outcome.

Earth time says you don't have enough time—eternal time says there's plenty of time. Let's learn to stretch our faith into eternal time to make decisions that affect earth time in the *kairos*.

Do you remember in Chapter 1 where I shared Albert Einstein's Theory of Relativity and how it refers to our "frame of reference," which is subjective to the viewer or the one experiencing it?

By faith we can make time appear to slow by controlling the speed of our soul. Slow down how your soul (mind, will, and emotions) processes by believing in faith all things have been completed already in eternal time and are just now being revealed in our earth time zone. Then you are in control of the present and within the eternal zone of the future where things have not taken place yet. *You* can do this by faith in knowing that God is already in the future, so we can rest in the present as we are moving toward the future.

If you remember the faith activations I shared with you in previous chapters, you can use that exercise again here. The farther away an object is in your frame of reference, the more in the future it is. As you walk toward it and it keeps moving away and you never reach it, by faith it remains in future and you remain at rest because you can't reach it in your mind or will or emotions. If your mind and will knows you can't reach it, two things happen. You either rest in the fact that you can't reach it and gain peace knowing you are actively living by faith and will be rewarded—or it frustrates you terribly until you catch it and you rush your soul in anxiety and fear to reach the goal. Choose to live by faith.

If you believe in Jesus and rest in who God is with His goodness and love and the good intentions He has toward you, then you can walk slowly to the situation with peace knowing you'll get to it in due time, in *kairos,* when earth and eternal time meet. This outcome is that your soul is in faith and control. This means you have overcome the curse of the fall because you have self-control and you're not guided by your natural eyes or temptations of your soul—rather, you're controlled by spiritual eyes in faith.

Time as an Illusion

Even the scientific revelations from Einstein can prove this as he says that "time is an illusion." It is an illusion to the believer and nonbeliever, but more so to the believer who knows the Word of God because we are privy to the fact that we are living in an illusion stronghold by satan to deceive us to believe we are in lack of provision, protection, acceptance, and our basic needs. This illusion keeps us in bondage and we lose our sense of control when we think we are losing our capacity to meet our basic needs.

Living by faith regains all that for us. The power of redemption can return our eyes back to the original design of "seeing" with *anablepo* and recovering the sight we lost in the fall. This new sight enables us to have the benefits lost by the curse of the fall and again rule and reign on earth.

Faith in Jesus's redemption buys back time that we can "feel" and sense daily in our souls. Try it now with a situation that you are facing that makes you anxious. Move it away from you and put it by faith in eternal time and see what happens. By your belief in God making it beautiful in eternal time, now you should rest and allow it to carry out on earth. Now your faith is producing a result, this result is endurance of your faith. This endurance by faith is real and can be examined, just like science, which has the power to prove our faith.

In this chapter, we discuss how to endure in your faith. The word *endurance* reveals whether we are really a Christian. As born-again, baptized in the Holy Ghost believers, we have been given the enduring power of the Holy Spirit, and God calls us to endure in all circumstances. Have you been overstressed and tired and working too hard and plowing the fields with no harvest? Then this is exactly what you need to learn today—how to endure by faith in the Kingdom. This revelation comes with a mind shift. You have to change your mind within your physical organ, the brain. We have to renew our minds, not conform to the world's pattern, and live within the redeemed perfect will of God.

Remember, you died, were buried, resurrected, ascended, and you took a new seat in the heavenly realms or eternal realms where time is everlasting. Jesus is seated at the right hand of the Father—and you are seated on His lap. That's your new place and that's your place of prosperity. That's your place of provision, wholeness, completeness, and fullness. The world is telling us all a whole lot of lies, but that's where the truth exists in heavenly places of redemption. You have a new proximity or place to live out of, and it is eternal.

The Word of God tells us specifically who we are, who God is, what God did for us to bring us back to that place of living in the Garden of Eden. Jesus redeemed us into the eternal realms of everlasting life. We may live in earth time while our body is on earth, but our spirit and soul are eternally tied to the heavenly realms in a new time zone which is like the Garden of Eden.

New Enduring Place

You can live in the Garden of Eden now because Jesus redeemed all things; He put us in His perfect eternal time zone, as we are living now in that ascension place with Him. Let's read Hebrews 10:34-39 (KJV):

> For ye had compassion of me in my bonds, and took joyfully the spoiling of your goods, knowing in yourselves that ye have in heaven a better and an enduring

> substance. Cast not away therefore your confidence, which hath great recompence of reward. For ye have need of patience, that, after ye have done the will of God, ye might receive the promise. For yet a little while, and he that shall come will come, and will not tarry. Now the just shall live by faith: but if any man draw back, my soul shall have no pleasure in him. But we are not of them who draw back unto perdition; but of them that believe to the saving of the soul.

You have a new existence from Heaven and the eternal time zone first. How then do you live and how do you respond to the world from your heavenly place? Even the author of Hebrews, whom I believe is the apostle Paul, says you *"have in heaven a better and enduring substance"* (Hebrews 10:34 KJV). He's speaking to both Jew and Gentile and saying there's something better and it's more enduring. And so that word *better* in the Greek is the word *kreitton,* which means "stronger, better, or nobler." It is broken down to the Greek word *kratos,* which means "dominion, vigor, power, and strength." See the key here? He says you have something better, which is *kratos,* which means "a dominion of power."

Kratos Power

Kratos power is not the same as *dunamis* power, which is "miracle working" power, and it's not the same as *exousia* power, which is "power of authority." *Kratos* is a power of dominion. It's a place or position. The author of Hebrews is saying you have something that is better, or a better place, and an enduring substance, or possession. The word *enduring* in the Greek is the word *meno,* which means "to stay in a given place, to abide, dwell, continue, or tarry." This means you have an enduring and a steady place now in the present while you are on earth in your body. But your spirit and soul are connected to a heavenly enduring place by the ascension of Jesus. When Jesus ascended, He took the church with Him. We are seated there in eternal realms, in spirit and our souls—our mind, will, and emotions. However, our body is here in earth time.

Now Heaven's characteristics are enduring and steady, orderly, full of giving. It's a whole fresh culture. You're a citizen of the Kingdom of Heaven. You have a better and enduring substance. You have a new dominion, a new place, and a "new and living way," as Hebrews 10:19 says. That word *substance* is the Greek word *huparxis,* which means you have new existence or proprietorship.

What I believe these Scriptures reveal is the author saying, "I know why you had compassion on me and why you're joyful in sending the goods, because you believe there is a better and more enduring place." This is a current enduring place of existence. It exists now in the eternal and is made manifest on earth because of what we believe. We talk about the heavenly realms because apostle Paul says we're seated there (Ephesians 2:6) and we have all spiritual blessings in heavenly places in Christ (Ephesians 1:3). Jesus Christ secures the fact that we have spiritual blessings in heavenly places that can be made manifest on earth now.

Isn't this exciting?! Through God's redemption of humanity on earth, we have now been bestowed spiritual blessings from Heaven made manifest now on earth by our faith in Jesus redeeming all things. The apostle Paul gives specific facts that everything we need is in the here and now. Jesus did the same thing because when He walked the earth, He said, "The *kingdom of heaven is at hand"* (Matthew 10:7). In essence Jesus was saying "While I'm here, watch the Kingdom of Heaven in operation; there will be signs, miracles, and wonders." Jesus is explaining that the culture of Heaven is entirely different from the culture of earth.

Jesus and the various authors of the New Testament are saying Heaven doesn't do things the way earth does things because earth responds from a revelation of bondage first. Heaven is a place where there is no bondage. They are saying, "Folks, shift your eyes. You need to recover your sight. Heaven doesn't look like earth and its ways of doing things." Stop viewing your difficulty as something that's not workable on earth. It's very workable on earth because you are seated in heavenly places and this means you have been returned now to the Garden of Eden by faith.

Earth time is death time, it is limited and a time zone that lacks. When all things were redeemed, when Jesus died, was buried, resurrected, and ascended, we went back to the original time zone, which is the eternal time zone where no death exists. This means we live in eternal time now and we are back in the redemption of the Garden of Eden. We returned through the "flaming sword" at the end of the Garden when we received Jesus and He redeemed the time. Now we live in an eternal time zone, and we can walk the earth like we're in the Garden of Eden.

Do you understand spiritually what is being explained? Don't look at Heaven like it's coming. Look at Heaven like it's here. *Kratos* power is being lived out in *dunamis* and *exousia* power; you now have dominion of miracle-working power and authority given to you because *kratos* power has been returned to you through the redemption of all that Jesus accomplished on the Cross. Why? Jesus fulfilled the entire requirements of earthly law and time to redeem us on earth, in the Garden of Eden, under a culture that requires an existence of faith and

Kingdom. It's a steady place. It's an orderly and giving place. It's a powerful place.

You may be tired, burned out, stressed out. There's a lot of difficult things going on in the world. Fear, anxiety, depression, loss can wear you out. Guess what? You can choose to live like you're in the Garden of Eden, which is the culture of Heaven and believe that you have a new existence regardless of what's going on around you. People who believe they are existing and enduring in faith and in His Kingdom are the ones who have the opportunity to see the blessings.

It is time to make a change today! I want that for you and your family. I'm sure you want fear and anxiety to stop tormenting you. You want the complaining to stop, the murmuring to stop. You no longer want to make excuses or have doubts. No longer saying, "God doesn't love me. God's not really that good. God's withholding this from me." You want to stop saying, "My life is so bad. God has abandoned me. God's rejected me." No He hasn't! None of those things are true. The devil is a liar. God did not abandon you—He never will.

God did not reject you. He loves you so much—so very much that He sent His Son, Jesus, to reconcile you to Him so you would be free of guilt and be able to engage in the culture of Heaven and ascension and in the eternal realms today. He loves you so much He redeemed all things through His shed blood to bring you back into the fullness that the fall and the curse took from you! Beloved, it can't get better than this!

Living in this place of Heaven on earth, our faith is active now in what we have from Heaven to be made manifest on earth. This new and enduring place is a new substance, a better covenant, a place where the culture of Heaven can be made manifest every single day. I want you to learn to live like that. What kind of place is this? It is place that the apostle Paul, or author of Hebrews, was excited to share. Hebrews 10:19-24 (NIV) reads:

> Therefore, brothers and sisters, since we have confidence to enter the Most Holy Place by the blood of Jesus, by ***a new and living way*** opened for us through the curtain, that is, his body, and since we have a great priest over the house of God, let us draw near to God with a sincere heart and with the full assurance that faith brings, having our hearts sprinkled to cleanse us from a guilty conscience and having our bodies washed with pure water. Let us hold unswervingly to the hope we profess, for he who promised is faithful. And let us consider how we may spur one another on toward love and good deeds.

Holy of Holies

Through the veil of Jesus's body, we now have the boldness to enter the Holy of Holies by the blood of Jesus. This is where the mercy seat is and the Ark of the Covenant in the heavenly tabernacle. We have been given boldness to go all the way into the outer court, the inner court, and all the way to the Holy of Holies. How? By the blood of Jesus. By a new and living way.

The Holy of Holies is the place in the earthly tabernacle and the heavenly tabernacle, where the high priest would go in and put the blood of the Lamb on the mercy seat, which is on the Ark of the Covenant.

From this place the high priest would declare that it is finished and that all sin had been forgiven for transgressors of the law. To enter the Holy of Holies, the high priest must come from the holy place (inner court) into the Holy of Holies. A veil or curtain separated these two places. Inside the Holy of Holies is the mercy seat and the Ark of the Covenant. When Jesus died on the Cross, this curtain was split in two to give us access to the Holy of Holies. This meant the power of sin, death, the grave, and the effects of lack of time were defeated.

When death is defeated, we regain time. Time becomes redeemed, as time represents no death. When this happened, the Word tells us that we now have access all the time, not based on our good works, but based on the fact that Jesus met the requirements of the sacrifice of our Passover Lamb and is the High Priest who has authority to make the sacrifice. Jesus is both. It is not by your works that you are forgiven or because today was a good day or because things are working well for you or because you didn't sin today. Things are made right because of Jesus.

New and Living Way

You are granted access to the new and living way because of what *Jesus* did. That's straight up. Hebrews 10:20 calls this the *"new and living way."* That Greek word for *new* is *prosphatos,* which means "to be recently slain"; and the Greek word *sphazo* means "to butcher an animal for sacrifice." And the word *living* is the Greek word *zao,* which means "to live." The word *way* is the Greek word *hodos,* which means a "road of progress or a journey, the route or act of distance."

So literally, there is a new and living way, which means if there is a new, there was an old way. What was the old way? There was, according to the law and the prophets, a way to forgiveness. This is where the high priest would go into the Holy of Holies and put blood on the mercy seat and declare that for the next year there would be forgiveness of sins. But this was only a declaration for one year of earth time—not for all time. It was a law set for an earthly time zone.

But our Jesus, our High Priest in a *new order,* a higher order, sacrificed Himself and declared once and for all that forgiveness of sin was forever. We have the High Priest, Jesus Christ—when you believe in Him, you have access for eternity. Jesus redeemed earth time and now eternal time. You now are indoctrinated into a *"new and living way"* for eternal time. You now have dominion or *kratos* power in a new time zone that encompasses eternal time, which includes earth time.

Earth time is inside of eternal time. Remember, earth time is death time, eternal time is life time or everlasting time. You are now a citizen of everlasting time because eternal time is the new order of time. That's why we have a new and living way because we have a High Priest who doesn't have to go in every year to the earthly tabernacle, according to Moses, which was patterned after the heavenly tabernacle.

Access to the Holy of Holies exists in the culture of Heaven being made manifest now. Jesus went up to the heavenly tabernacle, not to the earthly tabernacle. Now where are you seated? You're seated in heavenly places. Where has the decree been made that there's a new and living way in the heavenly realms? The courts of Heaven declare everything is final by the shed blood of Jesus Christ.

It is indeed a new and living way in the heavenly tabernacle that only He had access to, and He declared from there. The heavenly tabernacle is the real one, the earthly tabernacle was man-made. Jesus met the earthly tabernacle requirements, which made it obsolete on earth. Where now is the tabernacle on earth? Inside you! You are the tabernacle of the Lord, You are the temple of the Holy Spirit. First Corinthians 6:19-20 (NKJV) reads, *"Or do you not know that your body is the temple of the Holy Spirit who is in you, whom you have from God, and you are not your own? For you were bought at a price; therefore glorify God in your body and in your spirit, which are God's."*

There is no longer a physical temple in Jerusalem where the high priest in Old Testament went to sacrifice offerings. It was destroyed in the year 70 CE by the Romans.

The apostle Paul is telling the church at Corinth that we are a new creation of the new eternal order, with the Holy Spirit living inside us, and we are completely forgiven all the time. In eternal time never again will we be victims of time restrictions on earth. We are now citizens of a new and living way. Now you are called to draw near with a true heart in full assurance of faith, having your heart sprinkled from an evil conscience. Your heart is your soul, your mind, your will, and your emotions sprinkled from the guilt that comes from committing sin. This is inside your body. Your body and soul are the new temple of the Holy Spirit. You are now refreshed and cleansed, strong and washed with the pure water of the Word of God. In the book of Hebrews, this new and living way is also called the new eternal order of Melchizedek.

New Eternal Order

Jesus was a type of Melchizedek, or some theologians say He *was* Melchizedek the High Priest. Nonetheless, no matter which theology you prescribe to, whether He is or whether He is just of the order of Melchizedek, it doesn't matter, Jesus is the Priest of a new order, not the order of the Levites. He had his own order. He comes in as the High Priest. He was born of the tribe of Judah, not from the Levitical tribe. All these rules and regulations according to Mosaic law are part of the Levitical priesthood.

Jesus as the High Priest and in the new order of Melchizedek establishes heavenly realms to make a way for us into the culture of Heaven. And that is where He has positioned us, in a heavenly place where everything is declared holy, righteous, good, blessed, and honored in this realm. This is the new eternal Kingdom order, forever; it has broken the time code. It is not an earthly order based on the restrictions of earth time or meeting only the needs of earth time. It supersedes earth time and moves us all to eternal time. Eternal time is Kingdom time! Remember Jesus says that when He came, the Kingdom arrived!

We have been discussing having enduring faith. Enduring means an endurance of eternity, an endurance with no beginning and no end. Since you are now a citizen of a new eternal Kingdom order, you never have to go back to the earth for reference. Everything has shifted to Heaven now and will be ruled and will be moved from the heavenly places. Because this is the case, what needs to change? We need to change our thinking about proximity. Proximity is a time and place issue.

In this new eternal Kingdom order, all things are in eternity first. The sequence is eternity first and earth second. To endure, you need to know the power of eternity because that's your new space, that's your new place, that's your new position. From there, things are done differently. They are doing Kingdom business in Heaven. This is why they call it a new eternal order, because it's not done the way we've done business on earth. When God wanted business done on earth, He set up a system based on Heaven and then the earth failed the system. Satan got hold of it. Jesus had to free the earth and now we're set back into our original design. You may say, "Candice, that doesn't make any sense because earth living does not look like the original design in the Garden of Eden. I'm not living in some lush garden, and I'm wearing my clothes here and I have to buy and sell for my food. How does this make sense?" I will tell you how—it is all by faith.

Only faith can please God and God only rewards with benefits those who live by faith in the Word and what it says (Hebrews 11:6). By faith we believe that we are living in the earth zone in this present heavenly reality and the future heavenly reality, which means those of us who choose to live this way according to the Word are in the new eternal order of Melchizedek, which is a new heavenly Kingdom made manifest on earth.

We are going to see that a way has been made for us through Jesus to return and rule and reign from an eternal space and time proximity. Do you know He's coming back for a church that already lives the way they're supposed to? I know you think He's coming back to rescue you from your current condition, but He already did that. He did that when He died, was buried, resurrected, and ascended. He put us in the eternal Kingdom to be made manifest on earth.

Are you still scratching your head saying that doesn't make sense? Everything Jesus says is by faith, and He wants us to grab hold of it by faith. So how do we endure? We endure by faith. If you have a lack of faith, you're going to have a lack of endurance. If you lack in faith, you're not going to be able to run the race without getting tired. You're going to have continued pressures, continued issues. I want to encourage you to have faith in God's Word to be continually refreshed. You may be saying, "Yes, yes. Tell me how to live in the new eternal order of Melchizedek."

Tread Out Time

I love the Word of God because it has changed me from the inside out. Everything I'm sharing with you I live in my spirit and my soul in those places. It's where the grace of God is released in my life and where I can walk; I can tread in eternal time on earth. That's what the Word means in Joshua 1:3 (NIV) says, *"I will give you every place where you set your foot, as I promised Moses."*

That word *foot* is the Hebrew word *regel,* which means "to walk as a step, to endure in the journey and possess time." It means that you would possess time, that you would gain back everything that's been lost. Joshua is an Old Testament Scripture, but who did that for us in the New Testament? Jesus. He accomplished possessing time in the earth zone by meeting the requirements set by the earthly law to set us free from the earthly time zone to position us now in proximity to the heavenly eternal time zone. We regained time. When time is regained, everything is regained.

Hebrews 10:23-25 (NIV) tells us:

> Let us hold unswervingly to the hope we profess, for he who promised is faithful. And let us consider how we may spur one another on toward love and good deeds, not giving up meeting together, as some are in the habit of doing, but encouraging one another—and all the more as you see the Day approaching.

This new eternal order of Melchizedek is extremely important. It is active now whether you understand it or not. It's important to know how it operates; there's a power of enduring faith that is activated when we understand there's a new Kingdom eternal order. It is an order and alignment that God has called you for now, and it is the manifestation of the culture of Heaven and the heavenly realms on earth.

Every day, whether you realize it in your mind or not, you are living as a citizen in Heaven, where your conversation is in Heaven. You are bringing the Kingdom of Heaven to earth in this new order. In this place you can be with your brothers and sisters from a heavenly perspective. Remember, from here you're living and breathing and having your being, all that Jesus accomplished for you. We need to be preaching the completion of all things on earth by what Jesus did by meeting the law of Moses and completing the requirements of the heavenly tabernacle to shift us into the new eternal order and redeem time.

Many times in church circles I hear a lot of what still needs to be done. That means we're expecting the earth to shift based on how good we are or how much we have accomplished or our good works before God. This is exactly where the enemy wants us to be—Christians still under the curse of performance that was the result of the fall. If you don't realize that Jesus has already done it all for us, we will run ourselves ragged. We must tread out the truth of what has already been redeemed by Jesus.

You have to shift your thinking. Jesus did it all! And we're the recipients of His sacrifice. We have received the final stamp of approval by God based on Jesus—and from this we minister and share the truth in the earth realms. We have freely received, and now we freely give. Jesus took us back to the Garden of Eden and brought the culture of Heaven to earth, which is a Kingdom culture. We are His glory carriers of the eternal time zone on earth. What's our job now? To live out what's completed, then it is made manifest supernaturally.

Everybody wants a sign, miracle, and a wonder. We all want to see things begin to change. But how much are you believing and living as though it has already changed? "Has already" is a past tense term—a past *time* term, it means things have been accomplished already. Things have been redeemed already. Did Jesus do everything on the Cross for us in His death, burial, and resurrection and ascension? Yes! Are we really there or are we not? We are! We must live by faith that all things *have been* accomplished and met through the blood of Jesus on the mercy seat of the heavenly tabernacle on the Day of Atonement, which means you must position yourself to believe in the new eternal order of Melchizedek.

Time Redemption by Faith

What Jesus did is enough. It's not enough plus one more thing that you do. It is finished. When God showed me that the lack of time of my own life was redeemed when Jesus met the requirements of the High Priest when He went in and put His blood on the heavenly tabernacle and said it is finished and there is a new order, then I learned to rest because I realized I was on a new timetable. From then on, anytime I felt like time was slipping away or there was lack of time or not enough time and resources or whatever, I knew I was acting as if I was still under the curse.

But I know I am no longer under the curse of death; and therefore, I'm not under the curse of time. I am on everlasting eternal time, and He makes everything beautiful in His time and I can rest now and apply this to every area of my life. I can trust that what was written in the eternal truths of Jesus's death, burial, resurrection, and ascension cover and properly position me to live a new life in the eternal order of peace and rest and fulfillment, nothing missing or broken—only shalom, peace. Now because it's done, we can empower ourselves daily by shifting our belief to the spiritual realms and carrying it out in the soul or earth realms.

How much do you believe? How much do you want to see your faith shift your entire life into peaceful rest? Without faith, it's impossible to please God. He rewards those who earnestly seek after Him? In Hebrews 10:6 He tells us to hold fast to the profession of our faith without wavering. What is the profession of your faith? The work was finished on the Cross when the High Priest in the order of Melchizedek put His blood on the mercy seat and a new eternal order was started. And now you are to live the culture of Heaven made manifest on earth.

I encourage you to know that you're already living in the dominion of *kratos* under the proximity of eternal time in the heavenly or ascension realms with Jesus. God already catapulted you there. You don't have any more work to do to get there. The work you must do at this point is to believe. When you practice believing and exercising with prayer, reading and meditating on the Word of God, being a disciple of solitude and silence and simplicity, among other disciplines, then your heart is prepared to live in the heavenly realms.

It all starts with the initial belief that the work is finished, it was done on the Cross, and now we have a new and *living* way. It's not a new and death way. This is cracking the time code. If you don't understand the eternal way, then you don't know how to live the way God wants you to live. If you don't believe all lack is eternally finished, you don't have the power to live it out in the present. This is what satan robbed from Adam and Eve—the peace of God's presence.

Satan took them out of eternity and stuck them in a death realm. That death realm was defeated when Jesus entered earth time or death time. He paid the price; He redeemed it all. And now we're repositioned and able to assemble with encouragement and joy, meeting one another's needs from a realm of faith giving.

We must stop the enemy from lying to us about not having enough to give, and not having enough to bless, and not having enough to be all that God has called us to be. *The devil is a liar and he's been defeated.* Give him no more power by your lack of faith.

Prayer of Faith and Activation

I'm going to speak into your life right now in the mighty name of Jesus. "I thank You, Father, that You're shifting the dark lens off my friend's eyes right now. And this reader is going to begin to see You as You really are—the good Father with great gifts that come from above. The greatest gift of all was your Son, Jesus Christ, who turned it all around and gave us back eternal life. We thank You, Lord, for the new eternal Kingdom order of Melchizedek, the new and living way that enables us to live life to the fullest!"

Now as a faith activation of belief, I urge you to stand on your feet. Give the Lord a cheer. Give Him a "high five." Say, "Praise the Lord. I'm going to turn my life around today. I'm going to change and I'm going to be different. I'm going to see life differently in the mighty name of Jesus!"

Increase your faith by reading the Word of God. Get into His Word and pray to Him daily. You will live the culture of Heaven today when you do. I can see it. I feel it. Good things are happening to you. You're blessed to be a blessing. The favor of God is upon your life and God is getting ready to move you into major positions as you walk by the culture of Heaven.

6
SET YOUR AFFECTIONS

Set your affection on things above, *not on things on the earth*
(Colossians 3:2 KJV).

It is time to accelerate into the fullness of abundance, and I'm going to give you the good news on how to do that: *Set your heart on things above*. This is not some arbitrary statement. It's literally what God says in His Word. The apostle Paul understood the importance of setting your affections above. To see acceleration, our heart must be inclined to heavenly things, inclined to living in the realms of the ascension or the eternal realms. This is your real home, the eternal realms. The earth realm is your secondary home.

I want to share with you keys to step into setting your mind—your will and your emotions in your soul—on the things above. We always think Heaven will be such a great place, right? It has to be better than the earth realms. It has to be better than all that we're dealing with in this place; and true it is, but we need to learn to set the fullness of our soul into the realms of eternity.

In the book of Colossians, the apostle Paul was sharing this very thing. He was trying to teach the church at Colosse all about how they can position themselves for the greatest level of peace, joy, and rest, as well as the abundance that comes from Heaven.

Colossians 3:1-4 (NIV) reads:

> Since, then, you have been raised with Christ, ***set your hearts on things above***, where Christ is, seated at the right hand of God. ***Set your minds on things above***, not on earthly things. For you died, and your life is now hidden with Christ in God. When Christ, who is your life, appears, then you also will appear with him in glory.

The phrase *affection on* is the word *phroneo,* a Greek word that means to "exercise your mind or to entertain oneself mentally." Paul's basically saying, "Listen, this isn't some passive affection we're supposed to have when we come to know Jesus as our Lord and Savior." The apostle Paul is sharing a revelation he has received about exercising our mind. We must properly position ourselves to earnestly mentally and emotionally be in love with Jesus in the place where He is now and the place where He took us when we became born again.

Now you may wonder where is this place God took us to? When Jesus died on the Cross, was buried, and resurrected according the apostle Paul in the book of Romans, chapters 5, 6, 7, 8, we learn that we died with Christ, we were buried with Him, and we were resurrected in Him. We have been resurrected anew. Then the Word says that when Jesus ascended, He took us with Him to be seated with Him in heavenly places. That's our new place or position. We have residency in Heaven. We are citizens of Heaven, and so we must have a firm and fond affection for where we are currently living.

Ephesians 2:4-6 (NIV) reads:

> But because of his great love for us, ***God, who is rich in mercy, made us alive with Christ even when we were dead in transgressions***—it is by grace you have been saved. And God raised us up with Christ and ***seated us with him in the heavenly realms*** in Christ Jesus.

You might say, "Candice, but I'm not living there. I live on earth." Technically according to Scripture, Jesus redeemed you by pulling you out of the clutches of the earth realms and all the effects of that, all of the death and the lack that comes with that—and He launched you into a new life where there is a new revelation of things above. The Word of God is all about revelation and wisdom and knowledge coming from Heaven so we may grow in our understanding and soul transformation—so we are not conformed to the pattern of this world but instead to the revelation of the redemption that comes to us because of what Christ has done.

When the apostle Paul says, *"set your affections,"* or *"set your heart,"* he means for us to exercise our new place and position where we are actually living. Now you may say, "Candice, I'm living on earth and you have lost your mind." No, I have not lost my mind because His Word tells me that I am seated in heavenly places and that I'm a citizen of Heaven.

Philippians 3:20 (NIV) reads, *"But our citizenship is in heaven. And we eagerly await a Savior from there, the Lord Jesus Christ."*

That word *citizenship* in the Greek is *politeuma* and in the King James Version it's translated "conversation." My conversation, my community is in Heaven first. We are spending too much time trying to learn how to conquer the earth when Jesus already conquered the effects of the fall on earth. He has redeemed all things on earth and positioned us from a heavenly place of citizenship. Our job now is to believe in our mind what He did and properly position ourselves and walk in the fullness and completeness of the eternal realms.

You've been taught to press in and push through your issues, thinking this makes us real Christian warriors. That we must be pushing and prodding and toiling and doing all of that, but the apostle Paul says, "No, the secret is setting your affection, your heart on things above in the heavenly places." I realize it's hard to do this when we don't understand too much about Heaven, but the word *heaven* in the Greek is *ouranos,* and it actually means "happiness and peace and eternity." Our affections is where eternity is and exactly what we need to focus on in our minds and soul. When the Word says, "set your affections on things above," it means that the apostle Paul wants you to train your soul to live from being above in Heaven first and below in earth second.

Soul Explanation

What is your soul? Your soul is your mind, your will, and your emotions. Our job is to train ourselves to live above. How do we do that? We get into the Word of God, the Bible. And we train ourselves through spiritual disciplines such as praying, fasting, sitting in contemplative spaces with submission and solitude, celebrating heavenly citizenship with other Christians, and being in environments where we can worship the Lord. These are all things that help shift where we're seated on earth, in the natural, and shift us to being seated in heavenly places where our affection is to be now.

We move and breathe and live every day setting our affections on something. What do you set your affections on? Do you set your affections on family, on your job, finances, where you live? We put our affections toward things on earth all the time, but the apostle Paul in essence says, "I want you to set your affections on things above first and to exercise your mind spiritually."

So there's a little bit of work here. What is the work? You have to exercise your soul—your mind and emotions—by positioning yourself in faith. We increase faith by studying the Word of God, getting in there and asking the Lord to give you revelatory wisdom, knowledge, and understanding. I'm going to be praying for that revelation of wisdom and knowledge and understanding to be coming to you.

The apostle Paul grabbed hold of this revelation and he focused on setting his affections above first. He grabbed hold of it so thoroughly that he shifted himself to live in the heavenly places while he walked on earth. That's important because it means that Paul was having a heavenly impact in the earthly zone. We're called to do that all the time. We're called to bring Heaven to earth.

Now what kind of impact are you having in the earth today? Are you meeting the earth and its issues from an earth mindset or "ditch mentality of lack"? This mindset will drown you. Or are you meeting the needs of the earth from your proper position being seated in these heavenly places in the realms of the ascension, which are prosperous and full of abundancy? Who wouldn't want to set their affections on being above first? That will give you all the power you need to trot out the truth on earth.

Now the heavenly realms are also referred to as the ascension realms or the eternal realms—the place, region, or realm where God has called His people to live, even today. No matter what you're experiencing in the earthly realms, you are called to live in the places of eternity from the realms of ascension and the benefits of eternal time. This means you have to know and understand the differences between the eternal zones and the earth zones. What is this power? What is this understanding? What is this revelatory knowledge that God has given us that we can set our affections above? You can set your affections on anything, but if you set your affections above, you're setting your affections on something pure, holy, righteous, and full of abundance.

You may be thinking, *I just need a little peace in my life.* If that's you, let it be some "shalom peace"—nothing missing and nothing broken. The apostle Paul dealt with some of the same issues we deal with; but even more so for the sake of the gospel, he was imprisoned and flogged. He learned how to be content in both abundancy and lack. He is highly qualified to write the New Testament and tell us the secrets of living in heavenly places and setting our affections there. You may have your affections on your spouse or your children. Maybe a boyfriend or girlfriend or on earning money.

What if you put all that energy in setting your affections above and seeking God for who He is seated in those heavenly places with you? We know in Philippians 3:17-20 (NIV) the apostle Paul encourages the church at Phillippi:

> Join together in following my example, brothers and sisters, and just as you have us as a model, keep your eyes on those who live as we do. For, as I have often told you before and now tell you again even with tears, many live as enemies of the cross of Christ. Their destiny is destruction, their god is their stomach, and their glory is in their shame. Their mind is set on earthly things. But ***our citizenship is in heaven***. And we eagerly await a Savior from there, the Lord Jesus Christ,

The apostle Paul says he is crying that many are enemies of the Cross of Christ. Their end is destruction, their god is their stomach. The people were setting their affections on destruction, on what they want to eat, their insatiable desires, their affections for food and resources. He says their will even revels, glories in their shame as they boast about destructiveness. This is how people's minds are when focused on earthly things.

Paul makes a distinction, separating those who set their affections on things above versus those who set their affections on earthly things. He is referring to those setting themselves up for destruction, for shame, for difficulties, are those who set their affections on earthly things in the earth realms of death and in the forsaken time zone.

The apostle Paul says, "Church, that is not us! If we have come to know Jesus Christ as our Lord and Savior, we are citizens of Heaven." He is try to encourage us not to be focused on the earth time zone. Paul not only sees Christians in the earth realms, but he sees a realm of believers who have already passed on legitimately, as in their body, their flesh went into the ground and the spirit and soul went to Heaven, conversing. They're speaking, they're talking. You may think that your conversations exist only here in the earth realms, but as you speak even in earth realms now, Paul says you're a citizen of another realm and you are conversing there as well.

There is a living realm in Heaven being made manifest on earth. What we do here in the earth zone is a reflection of the eternal zone. There are conversations in eternal time. Every need is met there in the heavenly places. I endeavor to set my affections on where all of my needs have been met. The apostle Paul is saying, "Listen, church, get yourself to the right place. Set your affections on things above, this place of eternity, this place where there's no beginning and no end, and there's continual time with no death." He's saying that Jesus resides there in this place and because He does, the apostle Paul tells us in Ephesians 2:6 that we're seated with Christ in heavenly places. We are in Christ and Christ is there!

He also speaks of every spiritual blessing being ours: *"Blessed be the God and Father of our Lord Jesus Christ, who has blessed us with every spiritual blessing in heavenly places in Christ"* (Ephesians 1:3 NKJV).

How do we have these blessings if our body is only here on earth? It's not only that your spirit and soul are residing in the heavenly places with the Father—it's also a place where you receive the power that you need. There's nothing draining in the eternal realms. Nothing is pulling at you. There are no demands made. Everything you need has been completely provided. This means when you're called to set your affections on things above, you're called to position your soul in a place of receiving all the power and strength needed every single day to trod out the truth on earth. Stop seeing yourself with an earthly perspective. You need to see yourself from an eternal perspective and set your affections above first.

I'm going to break something off you right now in the name of Jesus. You're spending too much time looking at the natural realms and seeing only what's happening here. That is part of the curse of the fall, to only look at what is in front of you in the earth realms. You must shift yourself from that to seeing and responding in the abundant life that only comes by faith.

Remember, faith pleases God. We need to know that a key to living in these eternal realms, these ascension realms, these heavenly realms where we're citizens, we have to increase our faith. Hebrews 11:6 (NKJV) says, *"But without faith it is impossible to please Him, for he who comes to God must believe that*

He is, and that He is a rewarder of those who diligently seek Him."

Glory Realms Testimony

I have a testimony to share with you about setting my affections above. When God wants to release the glory in a meeting where I am presenting, I must look up—way above into the heavens to take my eyes off the earth completely. I must set my affections there only, with no look to gain in the earth. I must believe I am there in heavenly places and my affections are on Him and heavenly places. I am cut off from earth and have no eyesight for here. I must literally restrict my eyes from seeing what is in the room. I was in a meeting in Washington State, and the Lord called me to keep my eyes looking upward, He wanted to release His glory. I had to remain focused all through worship with my eyes peering upward, way up inside my head.

You can try it, close your eyes and look way up, you won't see anything but it will cut you off from your soul being in the earth realms. God says, "Stay here and don't move, I will bring the glory." So I began to pray and ask for Him to release the glory, but I never looked down, I didn't care if He did it or not, I just knew I was not to look down. When I finally opened my eyes, people were repenting and coming to the altar. I had to keep my focus up into another realm that I did not even have real sight for. I did not see anything at all, I just believed I heard Him and I did what He said.

He has since said that to me many times, and the glory has been released in those meetings and people were saved, healed, and redeemed. The eternal realms accessed by faith came forth and miracles were done in our earthly realms that were under the curse of the fall and restricted in every way. I set my affections above and God did it! If you want to learn to practice this more, just sit with Him in silence and solitude and He will do it.

Learn to keep your eyes up daily even if you can't see a realm, you are accessing it by faith and breaking all restrictions of death and time and allowing eternal time to come in and redeem and reset everything to a heavenly culture.

One of the miracles that came from this day was an immense increase in angelic activity. People saw and experienced the fire angels coming into the room. Fire filled the room and people were experiencing back healings, neck healings, etc., but they also experienced angels. You can read more about accessing angels in my *Angels of Fire* book.

The Soul Gains

When we live in faith and supersede the natural desires of the flesh to gain, we are setting our affections on things above and believing and understanding that what Jesus did is enough for us. I'm saying if you can grab hold of the teaching in this chapter, everything in the earth zone is going to shift for you.

Stop trying to work it the other way where you say, "I'm going to work it really hard here and wait to see if Heaven's going to answer." No, Heaven is where the conversation is, then that conversation comes to earth. We're called to care for what's on earth, but we're not called to be obsessed with what's here on earth. If there's something we need to be obsessed with, it's having our affections on things above.

You have to get into the Word of God and be washed with His Word. The Scriptures increase our faith, and when our faith is increased, we begin to live from the heavenly realms and see signs, miracles, and wonders. Who doesn't want to see a sign, miracle, and a wonder? Miracles happen when we focus our affections above.

If we're completely in love with Jesus, if we're completely in love with Heaven, have an understanding of eternity, and if that's where our affections are, heavenly portals will open that will change the earth realms. Nobody can change the earth realms without setting their affections above. First, you want to see order and alignment happen in your life and in your thoughts; set your heart on Heaven first. Then everything else will open for you.

You can set your heart on things above. When God gives you a word, a calling, a mission, a purpose, He makes it possible. When you read the Word, you get changed by the Word, and then you start to believe what the Word says. And once you believe, you're tapping into the uttermost part of faith, and then faith opens the blessings to come into the earth realms. God wants you to learn to live by faith. Matthew 6:33 (KJV) tells us, *"But seek ye first the kingdom of God, and his righteousness; and all these things shall be added unto you."*

Seek First His Kingdom

Seeking first the Kingdom of God means His rulership, His domain, the royal region of where God lives. Then to seek first the Kingdom of God and His righteousness means the right standing that we have with Him, the fact that His righteousness was given to us wholly and completely. It is a gift from God, the righteousness of Christ. Jesus says everything we ask for will be added to us. This is a powerful promise because instead of setting your affection on gaining something, instead of setting your affection or toiling to gain, you begin to till the land God has given you in peace and rest and He brings about the result.

There's nothing wrong with hard work. There's nothing wrong with doing what God is asking you to do, but guess what? You didn't get the gain because you worked hard. You got the gain on earth because you believed and you did what the Lord asked, and then He blessed you with it.

We can get stuck in the, "Let's get a reward from my efforts on earth" mentality, but that's not what God wants us to do because the earthly realms are death. To try and gain from a death realm only means toiling is possible, with no assurance of a reward. You must live from the heavenly realms to see heavenly results that come from tilling the land, not toiling in it. Toil means we are still under the curse. But Jesus broke the curse, so now we till or gather. All things have been redeemed and are now like Heaven on earth by faith.

When you maintain the mindset of trying to gain, as in still living under the curse, you will only waste your time toiling, working yourself to the bone in the death realms, and enough will never be enough. You'll never hit "enough" because this realm continually sucks the life out of you. It was designed by satan to do that, and when humanity got strong-armed by that, we were born naturally into a world that says "there's never enough." Therefore, you can never work hard enough to gain enough.

Toiling Versus Tilling

You have to set your affections, your heart, above, and you have to position yourself to seek first the Kingdom of God and His righteousness, exactly what Jesus has done for you. Then all things that you need will be added to you. Matthew 6:34 (NKJV) reads, *"Therefore do not worry about tomorrow, for tomorrow will worry about its own things. Sufficient for the day is its own trouble."*

The days are evil because they are under the curse of the fall, but God has redeemed our days by putting Jesus on the Cross. Genesis 3:17-19 (NKJV) reads:

> Then to Adam He said, "Because you have heeded the voice of your wife, and have eaten from the tree of which I commanded you, saying, 'You shall not eat of it': Cursed is the ground for your sake; ***in toil*** you shall eat of it all the days of your life. Both thorns and thistles it shall bring forth for you, and you shall eat the herb of the field. In the sweat of your face you shall eat bread till you return to the ground, for out of it you were taken; for dust you are, and to dust you shall return."

The effects of the fall is toiling.

The effects of the fall are told to us in Genesis 3:23-24 (NKJV):

> Therefore the Lord God sent him out of the garden of Eden ***to till the ground*** from which he was taken. So He drove out the man; and He placed cherubim at the east of the garden of Eden, and a flaming sword which turned every way, to guard the way to the tree of life.

The word *till* that is in the King James Version is broken down to the Hebrew word *abad,* which means more appropriately "to work as in to till or causatively to enslave or hold in bondage." It really is better said *toiling* as we know it. Whereas *tilling* in the dictionary English version means the "process to break up and aerate the soil for germination." *Toiling* in the English dictionary means to work extremely hard.

Toiling on earth is a form of bondage to sin and is under a curse. Which is what the Hebrew word *abad* means. This is what Adam and Eve entered through disobedience in the Garden of Eden. But now things have been redeemed by the "flaming sword" at the edge of the Garden, which is Jesus Christ who has brought us back to tilling from toiling. Jesus is the Flaming Sword in Genesis 3:24 that keeps the way of the tree of life, and anyone who believes in Him can now enter by faith into the Garden of Eden to till or gather and no longer toil.

In Matthew 6:34 (NKJV), we are instructed by Jesus not to worry about tomorrow, for tomorrow will worry about its own. How much of your life is spent on trying to figure out what's going to happen tomorrow or how you must prepare yourself for evil tomorrow? Jesus says, *"Do not worry about tomorrow."* What kind of living is this that our Lord and Savior says, "Take no thought for tomorrow." Aren't we supposed to be planning for the drought that may be coming? Aren't we supposed to be planning for the next terrible thing that may happen? No. I break that fear off you right now in the mighty name of Jesus. That's a life without faith.

I realize that if from a place of peace and rest, like the heavenly realms or ascension realms in faith, God is speaking to you about preparing for something, that is different from worrying about tomorrow or being enslaved to fear. Listen and obey from a place of rest.

If you set your affections on things above and you know that the goodness comes from God, that it comes from above to the earth, then you put your energies into Heaven—not in worrying—and then watch what God will do on earth.

I can see those blinders falling from your eyes knowing these truths. You were probably told you have to work yourself to the bone to get ahead. That's the only way you're going to make this life work. But the purpose of work is actually for character building and our character needs to be built. Our soul needs to be transformed by doing certain things, maintaining certain disciplines, because we were born into a world that was cursed—and work makes us purposeful and scared at the same time.

We need to know that the world makes demands on us and God disciplines us to get us into order and alignment. Every day when your character is trained, the kinks get worked out. God speaks to you and He is releasing wisdom and revelatory knowledge. You are stepping into the realms of His Kingdom when following His will for you. When Jesus speaks, He's telling people how their life should be, which is fully redeemed by Him.

Work because work is purposeful and it is good and because you are created to fulfill a purpose in the earth realm. Your work trains your soul, prepares you to be in proper alignment with God to receive from the Kingdom of Heaven and to receive from His righteousness. We have to retrain ourselves in every way. The apostle Paul knew this, which is why he says to exercise your mind and your soul. You're perfect on the inside in your spirit. Your soul is being transformed, and God is transforming you. Now, in the mighty name of Jesus, He is putting things in order and alignment, and the first order is Heaven, the second order is earth.

Faith Activation

Let's do a faith activation. I want you to again sit quietly before the Lord and meditate by saying the Word over in your mind.

Psalm 119:15 (NKJV) says, *"I will meditate on Your precepts, and contemplate Your ways."* Say, "I will focus on Your goodness, Lord." Just think of His goodness and that we are seated in heavenly places, our place of ascension and rest. All spiritual blessings are ours.

Sit quietly and rest in the fact that you are not to toil or gain. You may feel gain creeping up in your soul. You may feel the effects of the death realm in your soul, but just rest in His presence and His peace a bit. When you meditate and contemplate on God's promises for several days, you will recognize the struggle between the flesh, or the soul, and the spirit in this realm of death time. When you do, say, "Lord, take me forward to the heavenly places of ascension, where I have obtained all things in You. Take me to the Garden of Eden where there is no toil only tilling and walking with You as we work together. Let me graze and reset in Your pasture."

I encourage you to do this daily and you will begin to see the differences in the eternal realms and the earth realms, the differences between spirit realms of faith and soulish realms of the curse of the fall. Then remember that Jesus redeemed all things and you have power to choose to live in the earthly realms or eternal realms every day. If you want more practice, I urge you to obtain a copy of my *21 Days to Solitude of Soul* manual found on my website for more activations.

Prayer of Faith

Let us continue to pray and ask Him,

> *Lord, keep my eyes on things above and increase my faith every day. Let me see what it's like to live in this place and really receive from Heaven first. My life is turning around and my affections are set on You, God. I am beginning to experience in my soul the differences between lack and plenty. Thank You, Lord, for training me to live in eternal time and teaching me how I have all the time in eternity now—and I can now slow down and stop gaining and toiling—and start receiving. Thank You, Lord, I am cracking the time code by understanding supernaturally the differences between the earth zone of death and eternal zone of life in my prayer and solitude life.*

7
The Realm of Receiving

I would like to share a dream with you about the importance of the realm of receiving. On the final evening, I was in Finland ministering on the power of the eternal realms and I had a dream that I was in a war zone. I was trying to hide in the dark areas so the people coming after me would not find me. Dead soldiers lay everywhere in this camp, and I was there hiding. I saw two men acting crazy because they were so traumatized because of all the death. These men were existing in the realm of death. They were in bondage and pain.

Then I saw a great light come into the death area, its glow only covered some of the camp, not all of it. Where some of the men were hiding in rock clefts and formations, the light could not enter; these were zones of darkness. As I tried to find shelter and safety from this realm of death and chaos, I thought, *Where can I hide? Where can I go to be safe?*

I heard a voice say, "Hide in the light."

I remember thinking, I'll be found if I hide there; it's so bright the evil will find me.

But then I received a revelation, "NO—the light will be so bright the evil will never see me."

Why tell you this story? If you want to receive blessings from the eternal realms, you must come to the consciousness that where you are is a place of bondage and the only way out is to go into the light. In His light is where you will find eternal rest and peace and joy. In His light is abundancy to overcome.

There is a realm of receiving in the eternal realms, and we can access it by faith. Jesus cracked the time code with His death, burial, resurrection, and ascension; and because of all He did, we have been catapulted into the realm of receiving and rest. This is the place where everything is made beautiful in its time.

I encourage you to advance your understanding about how God wants you to learn to rest while you work. Work is a good thing. Work is a blessing. Proper work in the Kingdom and Garden of Eden is when you use your spiritual gifts and your personality and your unique talents and your testimony and your treasure and pour it all into the earth realm.

God does not want you to burn out, busted and disgusted while you're doing His will on earth. That's not His intention. Rather, that is the enemy's intention—to burn you out. In the dream, Jesus set my heart in the light of Him and His abundancy so I could survive the darkness and the toil that accompanies it.

Let's read John 6:25-27 (NKJV):

> And when they found Him on the other side of the sea, they said to Him, "Rabbi, when did You come here?" Jesus answered them and said, "Most assuredly, I say to you, you seek Me, not because you saw the signs, but because you ate of the loaves and were filled. Do not labor for the food which perishes, but for the food

which endures to everlasting life, which the Son of Man will give you, because God the Father has set His seal on Him."

Breaking the Curse

We find that Jesus is speaking to the people, and He says, *"You seek Me not because you saw the signs* [the miracles], *but because you ate of the loaves* [of bread] *and were filled."*

In other words, Jesus is saying, "You seek Me because I'm feeding you in the natural, but I'm not just feeding you in the natural, I am also feeding you spiritually as I teach you about the Kingdom of God—and as you learn, you realize that I am the bread of life. You want to know what this place is and you want to know how to live there. You want to know why I've come as Yeshua Messiah—because I'm going to give My life so you may go to this Kingdom place of rest and peace in your souls."

The people were intrigued.

I find the Scripture to be very interesting because Jesus says specifically, *"you seek Me not because you saw the signs* [miracles]." Sometimes people just seek after Jesus for miracles, but we need to seek Him for the bread of life that He provides. The Word is life and it breaks the curse of the fall; it breaks the lies over our thinking and doing. When you seek Him, you're eating from the Word of God.

The meat that endures to eternal life is Him, and He is the true bread of life—He is the Word. Jesus is saying, "I am the bread of life and I am filling you with the Word of God and you're following Me." Jesus taught before masses because He was speaking the Word, God's Word. Jesus is the Word of God (John 1). The Word brings hope, faith, and joy.

Yes, signs, miracles, and wonders are amazing and it's wonderful when we see that happen. But in this Scripture passage, people were seeking after God for the bread of the Word, and they were filling themselves up on that. They were gorging, they were advancing. He wanted them to follow Him for the Word.

Miracles were recorded throughout the Word of God. All kinds of amazing things happen, and everybody loves to see a miracle, but one miracle cannot sustain you. It might shift you into a new level of belief, but tomorrow another issue comes right along. You might easily forget the miracle that Jesus did. When He caused miracles, many people didn't even say thank you. We see that lack of gratitude with the miracle of healing the lepers (Luke 17:17).We can easily receive a blessing from God, but it doesn't mean we stick around.

You can feed off the Word of God every day, you can sit and read the Bible or you can listen to it, no matter how you choose to absorb His Word, it increases your faith and encourages you. It is manna from Heaven, it is bread we must live off and be nourished by every day.

Also in John 6:27 (NKJV), Jesus says, *"Do not labor for the food which perishes, but for the food which endures to everlasting life, which the Son of Man will give you, because God the Father has set His seal on Him."*

That word *labor* in the Greek is *ergazomai,* which means occupation. His statement, *"Do not labor"* means do not toil from your occupation or toil for your meat or where you get your meat. Jesus is saying, "You are following Me because I am feeding you." Jesus is feeding them (and us!) the Word that fills up and changes our soul. Your soul is your mind, your will, your emotions. The Word makes you love God. It makes you love yourself, and it causes you to love others.

Then Jesus says, *"but for that meat which endureth unto everlasting life, which the Son of man shall give unto you: for him hath God the Father sealed"* (John 6:27 KJV). This is the meat that He wants us to eat. That word *meat* in the Greek is *brosis,* meaning food, and broken down to *bibrosko,* and a verb *bosko,* which means "to feed or graze."

Jesus, in essence, is saying, "I don't want you to spend any more of your time toiling for that occupation or that food or drink or whatever you think you need right now. I want you to receive Me, the bread of life and the meat that endures to everlasting life." Jesus is saying, "I'm going to give you everlasting life if you believe in Me as Messiah and Savior. This meat I give endures to everlasting life and gives rest in My pasture." A pasture is what we are to seek after, as in Psalm 23 and like the Garden of Eden—a place of rest and peace. It is like the dream, the place of light and breath with no darkness or toil.

Jesus is saying, "Stop going about the daily routine, which is toiling to gain every day for food that perishes. Get off the cycle of gain and the treadmill of toil that wears you out, the same old fears of not having enough." It is time to break that by faith in Jesus redeeming us as sons and daughters of the King. He says, "I want you to come into the place where there is bread and meat from My table, which only I can give you. This is how you will survive and sustain an abundant, good life." He says, "Real life is receiving Me as bread that opens the door to everlasting life of meat and rest in My pasture. You must partake of Me and you will have eternal life."

John 6:28-35 (NIV) tells us:

> Then they asked him, "What must we do to do the works God requires?" Jesus answered, "The work of God is this: to believe in the one he has sent." So they asked him, "What sign then will you give that we may see it and believe you? What will you do? Our ancestors ate the manna in the wilderness; as it is written: 'He gave

> them bread from heaven to eat.'" Jesus said to them, "Very truly I tell you, it is not Moses who has given you the bread from heaven, but it is my Father who gives you the true bread from heaven. For the bread of God is the bread that comes down from heaven and gives life to the world." "Sir," they said, "always give us this bread." Then Jesus declared, "I am the bread of life. Whoever comes to me will never go hungry, and whoever believes in me will never be thirsty."

I pray for your faith to increase in this place and space. You may still be thinking that your bread is what you're toiling for, but Jesus says, "No, I give you your bread and your meat, your rest. For I am the bread of life." He means for you to rest while you are working because of what He has done. Rest in the pasture. Psalm 23:1-3 (KJV) says, *"The Lord is my shepherd; I shall not want. He maketh me to lie down in green pastures: he leadeth me beside the still waters. He restoreth my soul: he leadeth me in the paths of righteousness for his name's sake."*

Heavenly Habitation of Rest

Jesus says, "Work is good, but *till* what I have given you, don't *toil* it." Toiling is a result of the curse of the fall. We are to continue to work using our gifts, fulfilling our destiny, and doing the will of God on earth. And we are to do our work through the eyes of all things having been redeemed. Jesus is the bread of life and He is our meat, which means we have all we need and we have all of the resources of time, talent, treasure, and testimony that Jesus has bought back for us through His death, burial, resurrection, and ascension.

We are to learn to rest as our relationship with Him fuels our faith to believe we are in the Garden of Eden, or seated with

Him in heavenly places, and from there we have all the bread and meat we need. It is this way in the everlasting realms. It's this way in the Kingdom of Heaven. It is the "new and living way." Why is this so important? Because we don't understand the Kingdom of God. We don't understand the Kingdom of Heaven and its habitation of pasture rest.

Jesus tells us that every need is met in Him, catapulting us to this true place of existence now. All things have been redeemed because He met the requirements of the law and the new and living way, the new eternal order of Melchizedek. Because every need has been met there in that place and you are there, then all your needs are met.

John 6:27 (NIV) says, *"Do not work for food that spoils, but for food that endures to eternal life, which the Son of Man will give you. For on him God the Father has placed his seal of approval."*

Your work is sealed with the signet of the King—the time code is cracked and our everlasting life with time restrictions and lack and depravity has now been redeemed—it is sealed with God's very own mark.

In the Old Testament, God says He wanted to give the Israelites the Promised Land. This is about what God wants to give you too. It's not about how hard you're going to work to get it. It's about how well you're going to position yourself to receive it. There's a huge difference here.

Jesus says, "I have bread and meat that you don't know about. Stop thinking about the cycle of toiling you're in as a result of being from the generation of the first Adam—where the toiling and the stronghold of satan under the curse has created an environment where you think you have to gain something from it." Jesus stops this train right now with His death, burial, resurrection, and ascension. He was determined to meet the requirements of the law to take us to the place of peace with Him.

Since all this is taken care of, now we are only to receive what He intends to give. You are now a receiver of His meat, His rest, and of His bread, His provision, which is a sealed promise. Jesus sealed it so He would be the One who feeds us bread and meat.

This is the new and living way. This is the new eternal order of Melchizedek. This is the way that Jesus our High Priest bought for us when He went beyond the veil into the holy place and put His blood on the mercy seat and declared it is finished. He declared we are now receivers of the blessings of God. We would return to the Garden of Eden. All is redeemed. Because death has been redeemed and eternal life is in the here and now, all we are living in and all we do is filled with life.

It's a New and Living Way

If we're not living in the new and living way of the Kingdom, we're living far less than the Word tells us, and we are not receiving all the blessings God has given us through Jesus's sacrifice. A new and living way means living in the realms of the everlasting, a royal realm of rulership, in our present condition.

Although we exist in a realm of death, we can position ourselves in the realms of faith and fullness of life and eat the bread and the meat from this place.

In Matthew 6:25-34 (NIV), Jesus explains the parable of toiling and living under the curse of the fall, which He defeated when He died. He says:

> Therefore I tell you, do not worry about your life, what you will eat or drink; or about your body, what you will wear. Is not life more than food, and the body more than clothes? Look at the birds of the air; they do not sow or reap or store away in barns, and yet your heavenly Father feeds them. Are you not much more valuable

> than they? Can any one of you by worrying add a single hour to your life?
>
> And why do you worry about clothes? See how the flowers of the field grow. They do not labor or spin. Yet I tell you that not even Solomon in all his splendor was dressed like one of these. If that is how God clothes the grass of the field, which is here today and tomorrow is thrown into the fire, will he not much more clothe you—you of little faith? So do not worry, saying, "What shall we eat?" or "What shall we drink?'" or "What shall we wear?" For the pagans run after all these things, and your heavenly Father knows that you need them. But seek first his kingdom and his righteousness, and all these things will be given to you as well. Therefore do not worry about tomorrow, for tomorrow will worry about itself. Each day has enough trouble of its own.

Jesus says, specifically, "Why do you worry?" We are held in the mental bondage of worrying about what to eat, what to wear, and what to drink. Jesus is saying, "Stop the worry train! The Kingdom of Heaven has arrived. I am the Kingdom made manifest."

Let me tell you how the Kingdom of Heaven works—or how the culture of Heaven and its operation works. In that place, no one is concerned about what they will eat or wear or drink. Why? Because they know that God has sealed their provision through the shed blood of Jesus Christ. They know that they are there by faith that eternity starts when they received Jesus as their Lord and Savior. Born-again believers must believe that we are there now and our meat and bread is provided for us.

Jesus says in essence, "I want you to consider the lilies of the field and how they grow. They just grow from the ground. They don't do any toiling, nor do they spin." In other words, the lilies don't work, they just emerge from the ground as God intended, bursting forth in bloom. God's covering is over the lilies. If the environment is not the way it should be, the lilies die, right? But who takes care of the environment? Not you. God does. He brings the sun and He brings the rain water. He brings everything from Heaven that's needed for lilies to grow.

Jesus is speaking to the people and (paraphrased) says, "King Solomon in all of his glory was not dressed as grandly as even one of these beautiful lilies. If God can cause the grass of the field, which is here today and tomorrow is burned away, won't God clothe and feed us much more?" Oh, we of little faith. What's wrong with us? We don't believe God provides all our meat and all our bread.

Instead we give ear to the enemy saying, "You have to work harder or there will not be enough food on the table. You must sustain yourself; God will not sustain you. You have to do this or that is not going to happen." Listen, that is not God telling you to do that. That's the enemy who wants to run you dry. He must burn you out to nothing. Stop what you're doing; take a time out and say, "Lord, Your Word says that I need to have faith to believe You supply my meat and my bread. And I will stop toiling and start tilling what You give me."

To till is to rest while you are working, to fellowship with Him in the Garden of Eden while you do your work, and especially, not to worry about provision. He has already cracked the time code of death from your life and redeemed all things, so He knows every day and He is not pushing you—you are pushing you.

Prayer of Faith

Pray this prayer with me:

> *Lord, You supply my meat and my bread and it is sealed by the shed blood of Jesus Christ. I receive faith right now for your gifts. Your Word says, "Labor not." Lord, I thank You right now that I'm positioning myself to receive Your bread and meat of rest. And yes, Lord, I'm going to work as in, I'm going to go to my job. I'm going to bless my family. I'm going to do the dishes in my house. I'm going to clean my toilets. (Yes, you do have to do these things). But I'm not going to toil while I'm doing it, which means I'm not going to get burned out.*
>
> *I'm going to know that You're giving me everything I need to accomplish what You have called me to, by taking care of my family, taking care of my workplace, taking care of my church, whenever it is. God, You have asked me to be a steward of what You have blessed me with, but I will not toil like a slave in Egypt. I will receive the truth that Jesus redeemed all things and broke the time code for my freedom from death.*

Every day I encourage you to seek out and stand on this truth—God is great and He is better than anything the world has to offer; He loves you so very much and wants to bless you even more than you can imagine. If you can remotely think about the blessings of Heaven, they're yours. Not because of what you do, but because of who He is and how much He loves you.

Now sit in this place with me just for a moment because the Word says labor not, stop worrying about this and that. Your Father in Heaven loves you and He will provide for you. Matthew 6:33-34 (KJV) says, *"But seek ye first the kingdom of God, and his righteousness; and all these things shall be added unto you. Take therefore no thought for the morrow: for the morrow shall take thought for the things of itself. Sufficient unto the day is the evil thereof."*

Lord, I thank You for my reader friend. I thank You that at the reading of Your Word, this person's faith is increasing. I thank You right now that You are bringing to this reader's mind areas of toiling that need to be shifted to tilling.

God wants to set you free right now. He's saying, "You don't have to go back to that place. You don't have to keep doing that same thing anymore. You need to stop worrying about this. I'm going to bring you what you need. I'm going to bring you the meat. I'm going to bring you the bread. I'm going to bring you the clothes right to where you are."

I see it happening in the spirit realms right now. God is bringing you everything you need in the spirit realms. You may want to join me right where you are and cup your hands together and lift them upward as if you are receiving rainwater from Heaven.

God is bringing everything you need right now. Thank Him with me, saying, "Lord, with a grateful, thankful heart I thank You for Your Son Jesus who made a new and living way for me that I may receive my bread and my meat from You in the mighty name of Jesus."

Now you're receiving the blessings of Heaven. The Lord is raining down a level of faith as your Provider of meat and bread. You have all that you need taken care of because of the sealed blood of Jesus Christ who sealed it when He shed his blood.

Culture of Heaven Manifest

I think this is the hardest thing for us to understand. And it's supposed to be hard to understand because when you were born into sin, when you were born into the generations of Adam and Eve, you were born into a curse. The curse makes us think inappropriate and wrong ways about who God is and about who we are in Him.

From childhood throughout the rest of our lives while we're on this planet, we are consistently having to step into new understandings about who we are, who God is, what Jesus did, what happened when Jesus died on the Cross, and how that affects us. It's a continual learning process as we grow in our character and in our comprehension of the goodness of God.

To grow in your character means you understand how to trust God more. That's what character training is all about. God disciplines us and chastises us, so we'll learn to trust Him more. What Jesus is teaching us through these parables is that there is a new way of living now that He's brought Heaven to earth. Everything about the culture of Heaven is to be made manifest on earth knowing that Jesus through His death, burial, resurrection, and ascension sealed the deal that God is our Provider. You may think you're your provider, but you're not. You are just following through with your God-given purpose and destiny, but God is providing.

The following Scripture says it straight up as it is:

Romans 4:1-5 (NIV) says:

> What then shall we say that Abraham, our forefather according to the flesh, discovered in this matter? If, in fact, Abraham was justified by works, he had something to boast about—but not before God. What does Scripture say? "Abraham believed God, and it was credited to him as righteousness." Now to the one who works, wages are not credited as a gift but as an obligation. However, to the one who does not work but trusts God who justifies the ungodly, their faith is credited as righteousness.

The apostle Paul is sharing in this book of Romans that if Abraham were justified by what he did in his works before God, then he would have something to glory in. When we say we can do something, we can easily glory in ourselves. But Abraham believed God and gave God the glory, not himself. The apostle Paul is showing the difference between toiling (working) and having faith in God to provide as we till the ground we have been given. Abraham had faith and his faith was credited as righteousness by God.

Romans 4:4 (NKJV) tells us, *"Now to him who works, the wages are not counted as grace but as debt."* This means when we work, somebody owes us. If you work at your job, your boss owes you the wages to pay you for the work that you've done. So anytime that we're working to gain, we're positioning the earth realms to owe us something. This is not the culture of Heaven.

We work and those we're working for are indebted to us. You might say, "Well, Candice, how else does it work on earth? Don't we work to get paid?"

I say, "You're right, that's the culture of earth. But it's not the culture of Heaven. You live on earth, you have to work." But the key is, what's happening when you work is that somebody else has got to owe you something. But, *"to the one who does not work but trusts God who justifies the ungodly, their faith is credited as righteousness."* This is powerful—to those with the right attitude in faith while they're working, while they're doing their purpose and destiny, and believes on God being their only Provider, not the person paying you—that is the culture of Heaven made manifest.

Do you have faith to believe the person you work for is *not* your provider? You are only the receiver of the income; the one who receives becomes justified by God in righteousness through their faith. That's the culture of Heaven. In Heaven there's no buying and selling. Remember, the apostle Paul is teaching how toil works because we are under the curse of the fall. But thanks be to Jesus Christ who has redeemed us and placed in the new eternal order of Melchizedek. This is a Kingdom order!

We bring the Kingdom culture of Heaven to earth by having a mindset of faith where we bless with our time, talent, treasure, testimony, giftings, and all that God has given us—then in faith, because "I, God, am your Provider, you will receive from Me."

We must give God the glory and the credit for our work, otherwise, we will glory in what we're doing and it will become a gain, and someone else will be obligated to pay us. If we want to learn to live in the habitation of Heaven, we must do everything on earth like it's done in Heaven. Because there is no buying and selling in Heaven, an attitude of faith must be accelerated. You are to be a giver who gives beyond measure. You're a receiver not from another person, but from God. From this place of faith, you fulfill Scripture, and no debt is owed to you. God is returning to you because of your faith. I know, this is heavy revelation. We've been taught theologically so much about the differences between earth and Heaven but taught very little about how to live in Heaven and make that lifestyle manifest on earth.

Let us rest today knowing that God has now rigged the royal system to include that we are no longer hired hands—we are recipients of God's own goodness, grace, and righteousness. He will be our Provider and our Source. Give Him all praise today, for He is worthy. If you can begin to change your thinking now to believe these truths, you will build a new foundation of faith that will propel you ahead to a lifestyle of right decision making. You will no longer make decisions from lack or need, but instead from faith and prosperity. Do you believe?

Prayer of Faith

Lord, I thank You for my friend today who has been challenged to live beyond the understanding of the ways of the world and step into the ways of the eternal Kingdom's new and living way. Open their spiritual eyes and ears so they may see and understand the realms of Heaven and heavenly culture they have been translated to live into now. Lord, increase their faith so they walk in a realm of living faith daily, believing in Your goodness and love in such a way that they believe You are giving them the land to possess. All they have to do is believe it and take it! Help them to daily by faith hold out their hands to receive what You desire to give them. I thank You, Father, that You are magnified in the prosperity of Your servant (Psalm 35:27) and I want to please You by being a receiver of what You want to give me today!

8

TRANSLATED IN THE SPIRIT

In the prior chapter, I shared that you were now translated into a space and place of faith. This is a realm of the new eternal Kingdom order and heavenly culture. Our job now is to activate this and begin to make lifestyle changes from this new eternal Kingdom order. Let's learn more about how translation in the spirit realm can advance our understanding to live in a culture of Heaven on earth.

Do you remember in prior chapters I shared about Albert Einstein and his Theory of Relativity? Well, Einstein had another aspect to his Theory of Relativity—that time is universal. If you travel fast as on a plane, the slower time will pass for you. It is a small effect about ten-millionth of a second from those still on the ground, nevertheless, it affects our age. We age slower if we travel by plane. That's good for me with all the transatlantic traveling I do, continually crossing over time zones.

I have traveled through many times zones while flying on a plane. In February and March of 2025, I flew from Jacksonville, Florida, my home, to Detroit, to Sydney, Australia. Then from Australia to Auckland, New Zealand, to Christchurch, New

Zealand, back to Auckland, and then to Honolulu, Hawaii. Then from there to Detroit, back to Jacksonville, Florida. As you may know, when I traveled across multiple time zones going from the USA to Australia, I "lost" a day. This is really strange. Then I gained the day back when I traveled from New Zealand to Hawaii. My husband and I laughed because we thought if we lost a bad day, well, that's no problem. But what if we lost a good day, that would not be so good. Ha!

When we gained a day returning to Hawaii from New Zealand, we laughed and said, "I hope this day of March 13 is a good day, because we will have two of these days." We had two full days returned to us when we reached Hawaii. Not too bad to be in Hawaii for an extra day. At least if you time travel, make sure it is on a good day and not a bad day so you don't get two of them. LOL.

In this chapter, we discuss defeating time restrictions and the power of supernatural translation, or transportation in the spirit. You may think, *Candice, that sounds spooky. That sounds weird. Why are you talking about that?* I want to set the record straight on some things since many times people have the wrong understanding of translation and I want to give you some real good biblical truth and understanding on being in the Spirit of the Lord from one time and space to another.

You may know about Enoch who was translated in the spirit (see Genesis 5:21-24). Why was he *"no more"?* Because Enoch pleased God with his faith.

Community of Believers

People today are talking a lot about being translated. Biblically this is possible, but you must have a faith that pleases God. Believers are moving in the spirit realms, whether they are physically going from one place to another in their physical body or by dreams or by visions, there are various ways God can move a human from one place to another. But there is always an element of faith that's involved. When you start living in the ascension realms, living in the realms of faith, or eternal realms, this movement is possible.

When death entered the Garden of Eden, time was restricted. But we know that death has been redeemed because of Jesus's death, burial, resurrection, and ascension. So when time was redeemed, this caused us to step into new realms. We access those realms by faith that all things have been redeemed, even time.

If you have received Jesus as your Lord and Savior, then you have received the power of the Holy Spirit. When Jesus ascended, He then sent forth His Spirit to earth. In John 14:26-27 (NIV), Jesus tells His disciples that He must go to the Father but will send the Holy Spirit to us in His stead. Jesus says:

> But the Advocate, the Holy Spirit, whom the Father will send in my name, will teach you all things and will remind you of everything I have said to you. Peace I leave with you; my peace I give you. I do not give to you as the world gives. Do not let your hearts be troubled and do not be afraid.

Those of us who believe in Jesus as our Lord and Savior, we receive His Spirit into our spirit. In His Spirit, there is the fullness of who God is. Now we have been positioned to live within these various heavenly realms by the power of the Holy Spirit. These realms are like the Garden of Eden on earth before the curse of the fall. It's a place of peace, a place of rest, a place of joy. It's a place that the saints of God who believe in Jesus as our Lord and Savior have access to by His blood.

Enoch Pleased God

If you know Jesus, you are a saint, and you are part of His community of believers. This community resides in the realms of Heaven. We reside in the realms like the Garden of Eden, with nothing missing, nothing broken, everything full and complete. Enoch had a faith in God that launched him supernaturally to these places. Enoch had a faith that pleased God. For us this means we must live by faith that we are citizens of Heaven, and our conversation in faith says, "I believe I am a resident, a citizen of Heaven." Residents of Heaven will adhere to and adapt to Heaven's culture. What's heaven's culture? It's a culture of giving. It's a culture of resting. It's a culture of blessing.

It doesn't mean that work isn't done in Heaven; it just doesn't have the *toil* associated with it. There's nothing wrong with work, but working as in toiling means you're still operating under the curse—the curse that's been broken. Remember we have a new and living way to enjoy life.

Genesis 5:21-24 (NIV) reveals the story of Enoch:

> When Enoch had lived 65 years, he became the father of Methuselah. After he became the father of Methuselah, ***Enoch walked faithfully with God*** 300 years and had other sons and daughters. Altogether, Enoch lived a total of 365 years. ***Enoch walked faithfully with God***; then he was no more, because God took him away.

Verse 24 says, *"Enoch walked faithfully with God; then he was no more, because God took him away."* That word *took* is *laqach* in the Hebrew and means "to take, accept, buy, seize."

So what does this Scripture passage tell us about Enoch's character? He had a lot of faith and he walked with God. How? Where? That word *walked* is Hebrew from the word *halak,* which means "to walk as in conversation." This Hebrew word *broken down* is *yalak,* which means "to prosper." Enoch walked with God, conversed with God, and He prospered with God. He talked with God as if walking in the Garden of Eden.

If you are prospering with God, it means that you're already living in an ascension realm by faith, which is like the Garden of Eden. Enoch lived before Jesus; he was part of the fall, as is all humanity. Jesus had not yet died, been buried, resurrected, or ascended. Yet Enoch was grabbing hold of breaking the strongholds of the curse, of the fall, even in the book of Genesis, because it says he prospered and was acquainted with God. Abraham was in this type of relationship with God too; he prospered as he believed God and His faith was credited to Him as righteousness. There were many earthly saints who learned to prosper in the midst of living under the curse of toil and the fall.

Now because of Jesus's death, burial, resurrection, and ascension, He has taken us to all realms of prosperity where there is peace and joy and everlasting communion with the Father. Our God is a prosperous God and wants us to live in these realms by faith under the revelation that the time code has been cracked. Enoch walked with God, talked with God, and prospered with God. His thoughts were on God as the better of all things. He kept Himself in the faith realm. It was not a moment of faith, it was a realm of faith.

Faith Prosperity

Would you like to prosper with God and live in a realm of faith? Where by faith you are communing with God in the cool of the day in the garden? Where there is great prosperity, nothing missing or broken?

Hebrews 11:5 (KJV) says,

> ***By faith Enoch was translated*** that he should not see death; and was not found, because God had translated him: for before his translation he had this testimony, that ***he pleased God***.

Translation is not a difficult thing if you're already prospering with God. Being taken up with God or being translated or caught up or actually physically moved from one location to another means you have a faith that pleases God.

Now what is a faith that pleases God? A faith that pleases God is a faith that believes in the goodness and the love of God. It's a faith that believes that God intends to bless us and causes us to live in a realm of prosperity. We know this to be true because God sent His Son Jesus Christ to break the code of time and space and properly position us in prosperity.

It was never God's design that Adam and Eve would die at the hands of a spiritual and natural death and not prosper; however, they were convinced that they needed to eat of the tree of the knowledge of good and evil to gain something. I believe that Enoch was taken up because he did not live in a world of gain. It means that Enoch was able to defy his own needs for gain by living in a realm of faith with God, where he was completely and utterly dependent on the Lord, and God became prosperity to him. God is your portion and your lot. Psalm 16:5 (KJV) says, *"The Lord is the* ***portion*** *of mine inheritance and of my cup: thou maintainest my lot."* I believe that Enoch knew this. He knew the importance of being with God.

Translation comes from living in a realm of faith with the Lord, a realm where God is pleased, and Enoch pleased God. Let's go to Hebrews 11:5 (KJV) again: *"By faith Enoch was translated that he should not see death; and was not found, because God had translated him: for before his translation he had this testimony, that he pleased God."* That word *translated* is the Greek word *metatithemi,* which means "to transport, exchange, change sides, carry over." To change sides means to move places, from one place to the next. From one time zone or space to the next. From earth time to eternal time. From one realm to another realm.

Enoch had a testimony. What was Enoch's testimony? That he pleased God. How do we please God, we live by faith. Can you imagine having the faith of Enoch that he would be able to say that?

Do you think you will meet a lot of people today who know they please God? That's a level of enormous confidence to admit that, but clearly within Enoch's soul—mind, will and emotions—he was so unified with God that he knew God was pleased with him. And what was God pleased about Enoch? He was pleased with his faith because Hebrews 11:6 (NKJV) says, *"But without faith it is impossible to please Him: for he who comes to God must believe that He is, and that He is a rewarder of them that diligently seek Him."*

Enoch pleased God, and he diligently sought him. Let me ask you two questions: Do you please God? And do you diligently seek Him? Do you believe that God's heart is to reward those who live by faith? If you do, you are a candidate for translation.

Faith Testimony

People ask me, "How do you get translated in the spirit? How can you go from one place to another?" People have told me that I ministered to them in person or even in a dream or a vision. This means that God lifted me up at some point, whether a vision or dream, and took me somewhere. Now please know, in the case of Enoch, it was a physical translation. His physical body, spirit, and soul were relocated to Heaven. I was spiritually moved from one place to another when I was taken up to Heaven. My body remained in the earth realm, but my spirit and soul went somewhere else. You can read about this in my book, *Heavenly Portals: Creating Supernatural Environments through Heavenly Encounters.*

The apostle Paul speaks of "a man" in 2 Corinthains 12:1-4 (NIV), who was caught up to Heaven. We don't know for sure if he is referring to himself or not, but he writes:

> I must go on boasting. Although there is nothing to be gained, I will go on to visions and revelations from the Lord. I know a man in Christ who fourteen years ago was ***caught up*** to the third heaven. Whether it was in the body or out of the body I do not know—God knows. And I know that this man—whether in the body or apart from the body I do not know, but God knows—was ***caught up to paradise*** and heard inexpressible things, things that no one is permitted to tell.

That phrase *caught up* in the Greek is *harpazo,* which means "to seize or pluck"; broken down to *aihreomai* it means "to take for oneself, to prefer." So in this passage, *caught up* reveals that someone can be caught up by faith that pleases God, when God prefers or takes someone to Himself. He clearly took Enock to Himself. Remember the word *took* in Genesis 5:24 also means "to seize."

Born-again, faithful believers can have these testimonies. My testimony is that I live by the faith of God every single day, and I train myself to do the best I can to do that. I live by understanding that if I can't see it, it doesn't mean it doesn't exist. I live from a place of knowing that if God says it in His Word, it's done. One of the coordinates for translation is that we live by faith, a faith that pleases God and diligently seeks Him.

You may want to have a supernatural experience of translation. I'm going to speak into you that your faith would be increased in the mighty name of Jesus and that you would diligently seek the Lord, and I mean diligently from the realms of Heaven. You've ascended with Him. You sit with Him in silence in the Word, you speak in other tongues, you rest in that place and challenge your need for gain.

Let me expand a bit. People who please God are not always concerned about gain. They're not always concerned about where they're going or how they're going to get there. They're not always concerned about gaining something in order to fill a void inside them. They have a lot that they want to present and bless others with because they've received a lot from the Lord.

I believe when it comes to faith there is an element of need that one understands is complete. A lot of the needs we have in humanity go away when we present ourselves as living sacrifices to the Lord, and we just love on Him right there. We love on Him in a place of receiving, not a place of gaining or getting. You can have a heartfelt desire to be translated in the Spirit, and that's perfectly great. But I would say you need to work on your faith that you live now in a place of prosperity, not that it is coming. You live by faith in the eternal realms and not from the restrictions of space and time in the earth realms. Enoch lived by faith where he was literally translated. He was taken away. If we're going to physically be taken up to Heaven without seeing death, which is Enoch's testimony, then we need to be living in the place where the culture of Heaven and life already exists for us. We are living by faith all that Heaven is manifesting in a current moment.

You don't go from living in this realm and being consumed by death and expect to have your body translated and be taken up without living today in a realm of faith. Enoch was wholly taken up—spirit, soul, and body. This is because he spent his time living in the culture of Heaven, the Garden of Eden experience by faith. He became so consumed that it was very easy for God to cause him not to die in the flesh. His flesh was so in tune with Heaven that he lived until he was 365 years old. His flesh even defied the earthly time code.

Now today, I have never met anyone who's actually been physically moved where they didn't see death, where there wasn't actually a death ceremony for them. But that doesn't mean anything, whether I've seen or haven't seen it. We know that happened to Enoch.

However, I, like other people I know from the supernatural and spiritual side of things, have been moved in my dreams and in my visions and in my quiet times with the Lord to other destinations to do the work of the ministry or to bless others, to carry that prosperity to another place, to make a deposit. When I was caught up to Heaven, there was no time restriction where I went. When I returned, I had been gone about 45 minutes in earth time, but it felt like I had never left and no time had passed, that was the reality of the eternal time zone that I was catapulted into.

You may be having the same type of experiences. I have awakened from a dream after traveling to various nations to minister to people. Or I've gone over there and blessed somebody here. If you have had a similar experience, it's because you are already learning to live in the realms of the ascension, the heavenly and eternal realms with no time and space issues. This is becoming such a lifestyle for you that God is shifting you in your dreams and in your visions, in your quiet time with Him to other places.

Today, you can pray for God to take you to these places in the spirit realms. God may shift you that way spiritually, where you carry a large burden for another nation and you start being shifted to another nation before you even get there and you start praying and interceding. That's a form of translation in the spirit. But the translation in the Bible is specific to the fact that Enoch did not see death. He was physically moved from one place to another in the flesh.

Testimony of Translation

So in addition to my out-of-body experience when I was caught up to Heaven, I have had many translation experiences; and one specifically comes to my mind. God had spoken to me about going to Greece and Turkey to minister. I had this on my heart for months; I had encountered God through a few different ways to know that I should go. I was waffling in making plans to go and said, "Lord, if You want to me to go on this trip, I need to see myself there. Take me into the future so I know I am to be there."

That night I went to bed and I had multiple dreams, one of them was my walking in the ancient ruins of Turkey. I knew when I woke up that God was revealing that it was written in His will for my life. I also had that same night a dream encounter when I told God, "I need more faith for what You are asking me to do," and I saw in the dream some people sowing a money seed in faith so they could get a breakthrough. I also saw a ministry leader in the dream and I believed I was to sow a financial seed into this person's ministry for the breakthrough. So when I woke from the dream, I sowed a seed into the ministry. I also made plans that day to buy a plane ticket to Greece.

What does this mean? God translated me into what the eternal realms had already written about my life. He led me by a dream to walk in the ruins of Greece and Turkey so that I would know I was supposed to go.

When we talk about needing a breakthrough, to sum that up it means I needed my faith for the eternal to be made manifest on earth. We don't need breakthroughs in the eternal realm, we need them in the earth realm so we can step fully into the eternal realms. I needed a breakthrough for my purpose, or destiny.

This is why if we spend more time in the eternal realms by faith, we won't need breakthrough. I had been struggling between the two realms. I had been waffling between belief and unbelief. I needed to get on the eternal side where it was written I was to go, and then I sowed a financial seed in faith and it was done!

Philip Was Translated

Now I want to talk about Philip who is mentioned in the New Testament, not the Old Testament. Enoch's experiences were in the Old Testament but spoken about in the New Testament and given equity by an understanding that he pleased God and that he diligently sought the Lord, conversed and walked with God in a place of prosperity. That place of prosperity is in the ascension, or eternal realms.

Philip actually moved from one place to another. It wasn't about his death, it was about him doing ministry from one place to another.

The Word says in Colossians 1:12-14 (NKJV):

> Giving thanks to the Father who has qualified us to be partakers of the inheritance of the saints in the light. He has delivered us from the power of darkness and

> conveyed us into the kingdom of the Son of His love, in whom we have redemption through His blood, the forgiveness of sins.

Technically, all of us were translated from darkness into light when we believed in Jesus as our Lord and Savior. That word *translation* is the same word that we find in Hebrews 11 when we talk of Enoch's translation. It means "to change sides or time zones or spaces." There are many realms in Heaven as Ephesians 1:3 (NKJV) reveals we have been blessed, *"with every spiritual blessing in the heavenly* ***places*** *in Christ."* This is also mentioned in Ephesians 1:20; 2:6; 3:10; and 6:12. There are many mentions of heavenly realms or spaces. We have in heavenly places, spaces of time that are eternal realms, faith realms, ascension realms, prosperity realms, angelic realms, etc.

Translation is something that happened to all of us when we left the kingdom of darkness, believing in Jesus as our Lord and Savior, and walked into the Kingdom of Light. Translation is not spooky, it is part of the transfer we make from the realms of darkness or death or earth time zones, to the realms of light and eternity, the eternal realms of no death ever. This means we translated time zones.

If you have not received Jesus as your Lord and Savior, now is time to do so, so you can translate time zones too. Let me lead you in this prayer, "Father, forgive me for I have sinned and I want to know Your forgiveness and receive salvation through Your Son, Jesus Christ." When you believe and confess with your mouth Jesus Christ as Lord, you are saved and now translated to the Kingdom of God—the Kingdom with no end, no beginning and no end. It is eternal.

What was enough to translate Enoch and us and what pleases God? Our faith.

Now, let's talk about Philip. Acts 8:26-40 (NKJV) tells us:

> Now an angel of the Lord spoke to Philip, saying, "Arise and go toward the south along the road which goes down from Jerusalem to Gaza." This is desert. So he arose and went. And behold, a man of Ethiopia, a eunuch of great authority under Candace the queen of the Ethiopians, who had charge of all her treasury, and had come to Jerusalem to worship, was returning. And sitting in his chariot, he was reading Isaiah the prophet. Then the Spirit said to Philip, "Go near and overtake this chariot."
>
> So Philip ran to him, and heard him reading the prophet Isaiah, and said, "Do you understand what you are reading?"
>
> And he said, "How can I, unless someone guides me?" And he asked Philip to come up and sit with him. The place in the Scripture which he read was this:
>
> "He was led as a sheep to the slaughter;
> And as a lamb before its shearer is silent,
> So He opened not His mouth.
> In His humiliation His justice was taken away,
> And who will declare His generation?
> For His life is taken from the earth."
>
> So the eunuch answered Philip and said, "I ask you, of whom does the prophet say this, of himself or of some other man?" Then Philip opened his mouth, and beginning at this Scripture, preached Jesus to him. Now as they went down the road, they came to some water. And the eunuch said, "See, here is water. What hinders me from being baptized?"

> Then Philip said, "If you believe with all your heart, you may."
>
> And he answered and said, "I believe that Jesus Christ is the Son of God."
>
> So he commanded the chariot to stand still. And both Philip and the eunuch went down into the water, and he baptized him. Now when they came up out of the water, the Spirit of ***the Lord caught Philip away***, so that ***the eunuch saw him no more***; and he went on his way rejoicing. But ***Philip was found at Azotus***. And passing through, he preached in all the cities till he came to Caesarea.

The eunuch asked Philip to tell him who he was reading about. Philip begins with the very passage of Scripture that tells the good news about Jesus, the One who was taken from the earth (Acts 8:33). God had asked Philip to go to this place to minister, to affirm for the eunuch that he was reading about Jesus being taken from the earth. As they traveled along the road, they came to some water and the eunuch received Jesus and he wanted to be baptized. Philip baptized him; when the eunuch came up out of the water, the Spirit of the Lord suddenly "caught Philip away" in his spirit, soul, and body. So much so, that the eunuch didn't see him again.

Philip was a man translated in the physical in the New Testament, and the eunuch rejoiced and walked away because he was saved and baptized. Verse 40 says, *"But Philip was found at Azotus. And passing through, he preached in all the cities till he came to Caesarea."* What's exciting here is that Philip accomplished his purpose and was then taken to another space and another place.

So what do we learn here? We learn from this passage concerning Philip that you must serve your purpose, and once you do that in faith, then God can take you to the next place. That's as much true in the natural as it is in the spiritual. Translation means living by faith and accomplishing purpose. It takes faith to believe God and obey the purpose you have been sent to accomplish.

Where's Your Faith

So what is important to know about translation? You have to have a faith that pleases God; you have to seek Him diligently; and you have to be doing or completed your purpose. You have to obey the Lord by faith. Philip was willing and he was obedient. He accomplished his purpose by helping the eunuch understand that Jesus died, was resurrected, ascended, and defeated death to save all who believe. The eunuch wanted to know more about Jesus taken from the earth, as recorded in Acts 8:33 (KJV): *"for his life is taken from the earth."*

I hope you see that God was prepared for a divine setup. Philip and the eunuch had been reading about Jesus and His ascension. And then what does the eunuch see happen to Philip? Philip was taken from the place where they were.

I believe that passage also proves to the eunuch that his salvation was sealed through Jesus's sacrifice—and also to Philip, that he had completed his purpose and now he was moved to another place. God does everything, causes everything, defies any natural law on the earth to see His perfect will completed. God can make your body physically go from one place to another, or God can move you in dreams or visions—whatever He deems necessary to accomplish your God-given destiny. You were born for purpose before any day actually happened (Psalm 139:16).

Prayer of Faith

So let me pray with you right now.

> *Lord, I thank You, that You've stirred our spirits in regard to translation. You are affirming our need for a faith increase for signs, miracles, wonders, and for translation in the spirit. We ask for dreams and visions and physical relocations where we go to other nations and places to meet with people by faith and to accomplish the purpose for which You sent us. Open our hearts to live in the realms of faith like Enoch and Philip, that we may please You with our faith. We thank You for the opportunity to be translated into the Kingdom of Life where we now live in the eternal realms. We will not die a spiritual death; and at Your call, if You take us up, we will go in spirit, soul, and body at Your word.*

9

Recover Your Sight

Einstein apparently had another concept that he considered important in his understanding of time—the "block universe." In this revelation, "all events that have occurred and have yet to occur already exist." It is again a subjective experience of how time flows. This means space and time flow as a single unit where a series of events occur that is not really there; this brings an order of events in time that were destined to happen anyway.

Maybe this is like what Joshua experienced in Joshua 10:12-14 (KJV):

> Then spake Joshua to the Lord in the day when the Lord delivered up the Amorites before the children of Israel, and he said in the sight of Israel, Sun, stand thou still upon Gibeon; and thou, Moon, in the valley of Ajalon. And the sun stood still, and the moon stayed, until the people had avenged themselves upon their enemies. Is not this written in the book of Jasher? So the sun stood still in the midst of heaven, and hasted not to go down about a whole day. And there was no day like that before

> it or after it, that the Lord hearkened unto the voice of a man: for the Lord fought for Israel.

The sun and moon stood still until Joshua finished the task God called him and the people of Israel to do. Maybe it was meant to happen all along and written, then Joshua stepped into it and God did a miracle. I am only speculating, but that is what it is like with the supernatural. We believe, and it comes to pass in the natural.

In this chapter, I share my insights about breaking strongholds of lack, strongholds of poverty, depravity of your soul, and coming out from under the curse of the fall. Jesus died, was buried, resurrected, and ascended to defeat the curse and the *kratos* or dominion power of sin, death, and the grave. He defeated the strongholds the enemy had upon us in regard to lack, poverty, and depravity.

One of the keys to walking in our freedom is to see things differently. We are called to see as God sees, we are called to see in the spirit. We are called to see from the eyes of prosperity, with the curse of toil being released from our life.

There are two different ways to see things that are very easy to understand. In Matthew 13:13-16 (NIV), Jesus says:

> This is why I speak to them in parables: ***Though seeing, they do not see; though hearing, they do not hear or understand.*** In them is fulfilled the prophecy of Isaiah: "You will be ever hearing but never understanding; you will be ever seeing but never perceiving. For this people's heart has become calloused; they hardly hear with their ears, and they have closed their eyes. Otherwise they might see with their eyes, hear with their ears, understand with their hearts and turn, and I would heal

them." But blessed are your eyes because they see, and your ears because they hear.

Spiritual Sight

Jesus is showing us specifically in the parables that there are two different ways to see and two different ways to hear. I want to help you understand the differences between the two types of "seeing" that Jesus is talking about.

When we talk about our current vision in the earthly realms, this is sight through the lens of the fall—we see through a cursed lens of earthly time and resources with all its darkness, heaviness, and lies. This is called seeing in the natural. Jesus says in essence in Matthew 13:13-14: "I talk in parables so I can expose those who are not Mine yet, because they all see and hear a certain way." Jesus understands humanity and how humans see and hear in the natural. He knows we are under a curse until we know Him—until then, our eyes and ears are natural and earthly and reflect life as only depraved, lost, poor, sick, etc.

So in Matthew 13:13-14, Jesus begins to expose them to the difference between their natural eyesight and hearing—and their born-again new way of life.

There are two specific Greek words that reveal lack and depravity. The first word *seeing* refers to the earthly realm and is the Greek word *blepo,* which means "to behold or beware." It refers to the quick, fast images that we see in the earth realm—images without much thought, just a lot of fluff. Sound familiar with most of what the media is feeding us these days?

For example, if I'm on TikTok, I don't usually stop scrolling until something grabs my attention. Otherwise, I just keep on going. I believe that in this parable Jesus is saying that type of seeing is not appropriate, saying, *"Though seeing, they do not see...."* He is saying they need salvation to see properly all that His Father has given them. This reveals the prophet Isaiah's prophecy that *"'You will be ever hearing but never understanding; you will be ever seeing but never perceiving."*

So this means there is another way of seeing, which is perceiving. What is this perceiving that happens to a believer? Let's fast-forward to Matthew 13:15 (NIV), *"For this people's heart has become calloused; they hardly hear with their ears, and they have closed their eyes. Otherwise they might see with their eyes, hear with their ears, understand with their hearts and turn, and I would heal them."*

So according to this parable, all of us before we received Jesus, our hearts are waxed gross, which means we are calloused or hardheaded and can only see naturally from the place of depravity and the curse of the fall. However, we may at any moment have our souls open to receive Jesus and become converted; and when we do, we enter covenant with God, become His son or daughter, and we see and hear differently.

Now let's go back to the beginning of Matthew 13:14 (NIV), *"You will be ever hearing but never understanding; you will be ever seeing but never perceiving."* These are people who are looking but not seeing spiritually. Instead, they are seeing less than or from the eyes of the curse. Rather, they should be perceiving. *Perceive* is the Greek word *eido,* which is pronounced I-DO as in making a covenant. When you say your marriage vows you say, "I do," agreeing with the commitment and unity that is marriage.

So, we as Kingdom dwellers and the sons and daughters of the King are to have an *eido* or covenant perspective when we come to know Jesus and receive Him as our Lord and Savior. We move from seeing in the natural *(blepo)* to perceiving as in the spiritual *(eido). Blepo* is how we see because of the curse of the fall. We see with no spiritual thought; we are blind because we only see naturally through the eyes of deception where everything is lack and poverty and we think we must gain something to have something.

Jesus is saying that when we come to know Him, we have access to our spiritual, covenant sight, our *eido* sight. Before we are born again in Jesus, we have a mindless way of seeing things, we are under curse. But once we become born again and our sins are forgiven, we now move to a place of spiritual perception, covenant, *eido* sight—we see in the spirit.

Spiritual Hearing

This same natural-versus-spiritual perspective affects our hearing.

Let's read Matthew 13:15 (NIV) to "see" what Jesus says about "hearing":

> For this people's heart has become calloused; they hardly ***hear*** with their ears, and they have closed their eyes. Otherwise they might see with their eyes, hear with their ears, understand with their hearts and turn, and I would heal them.

Hear in the natural is the Greek word *akouo,* which means "to hear noise." It is much like white noise. When we are born into the earth, we hear *akouo,* an earthly hearing from the curse of the fall. It's like when you turn off the television and sometimes you're greeted with a blank screen and white noise.

Or maybe you have white noise machine? My daughter, who has three young children, has a white noise machine near the baby's crib. It displays various soft-color lights and makes a terribly annoying sound, in my opinion. I have no idea how our granddaughters can rest hearing that sound, yet they are sound asleep within minutes.

To me it is annoying, but that's because I've moved from *akouo,* which is white noise, to a place of the Greek word *suniemi,* which means "to send, put together, comprehend, act piously, consider and be wise." *Suniemi* means to understand from a spiritual perspective and also means a covenant relationship has been made with the Lord.

So there's two different forms of seeing and two different forms of hearing. Why is this important? Because every single day you're going to be challenged as to whether or not you're going to use your spiritual senses to see and hear from an earthly depraved standpoint under the curse—or from a heavenly eternal perspective of all things redeemed by the death, burial, resurrection, and ascension of Jesus.

Hebrews 5:10-14 (NKJV) reads:

> Called by God as High Priest "according to the order of Melchizedek," of whom we have much to say, and hard to explain, since you have become dull of hearing. For though by this time you ought to be teachers, you need someone to teach you again the first principles of the oracles of God; and you have come to need milk and not solid food. For everyone who partakes only of milk is unskilled in the word of righteousness, for he is a babe. But solid food belongs to those who are of full age, that is, those who by reason of use have their ***senses*** exercised to discern both good and evil.

Senses in the Greek is *aistheterion,* which means "proper perception." It is an advancement of the spiritual sight that comes from *eido* covenant relationship. We must practice and exercise this level of spiritual sensing, as it does not come automatically. We must accept and continually acknowledge the truth that all things are redeemed and that everything that was stolen in the curse Jesus bought back for us.

It is necessary to remember that Jesus is the High Priest in the order of Melchizedek for our faith to increase and our senses to be activated. This truth gives us the power to know we have been given an endless life and all time has been redeemed as part of our covenant relationship with Jesus.

Jesus met the requirements set in the earth realms so that all things are now redeemed and we can return to the Garden of Eden where our spiritual sight and hearing would indeed be correct. To be Kingdom citizens who fully experience the benefits of what Jesus did, we must activate our spiritual eyes and ears to discern both good and evil. That word *good* in the Greek is *kalos* and means "beautiful."

Remember, Jesus makes all things beautiful in His time, which is everlasting time. We must be in the correct time zone by faith, which is eternal time. That word *evil* in the Greek is *kakos* and means "effects of depravity." Wow, we are able to discern what has been redeemed and made beautiful and will continue to be made beautiful in His eternal time—and we can discern what is evil or depraved and is of the devil. We need to know when we are lacking in faith and acting as if things are not redeemed. We must not respond with depraved minds, which means without faith of the full redemption of Jesus Christ.

It is so important we live confidently knowing that all things are redeemed already. Remember Ephesians 5:16-17 (NKJV) which says, *"Redeeming the time, because the days are evil. Therefore do not be unwise, but understanding what the will of the Lord is."*

Redeeming in the Greek is the word *exagorazo,* which means "to rescue from loss." Jesus rescued us from loss, the High Priest in the order of Melchizedek, when He came into the earth realms and died on the Cross and put His blood on the mercy seat and declared it is finished—as in a set time in the earth zone, all things would now be redeemed on earth for eternity.

As mentioned previously, this redemption is of "time," in the Greek it's *kairos* or the proper time occasions happen in earth time only. They are set in eternal time, but when they approach in earth time they become proper time on earth to be redeemed in earth time. Time does not have to be redeemed in Heaven because there is no evil there. The word *days* in the Greek is *hemera,* which means the time and space between dawn and dark, which is also earthly. This whole Scripture is about how earth time is redeemed. Because earth time is now redeemed, we should be living like it.

As a result of earth time and all earthly resources now being redeemed by our High Priest, Yeshua Messiah, in the order of Melchizedek, will you see and hear in the spiritual, or will you see and hear in the natural? This is your choice by faith. In other words, do you believe you are saved from the curse and your sight and hearing have been redeemed and you now choose to function from the spiritual perspective of eternal realms?

Redemption is so amazing because the devil loses his power when we gain back time and its resources. When we no longer are in depravity in our senses, the evil one loses all control over our souls to cause us distress and to lose hope. We can now live as though the fall and the curse never happened. We can live completely victorious on earth!

Whenever we see and hear in the natural—the negativity and bondage of depravity that comes from the curse of the fall—we can instantly choose to say, "This is not right! I must see and hear spiritually as Jesus redeemed all things by His blood. I am under the power of the endless life and the new and living way of the order of Melchizedek."

The enemy tests us to see if we will submit to the Lord and follow the new and living Kingdom way made manifest for us by Jesus's death, burial, resurrection and ascension. Choose life!

The best part of redemption is that now you truly have freedom of choice. Think on that revelation truth for a moment. Because Jesus set us free from the curse of the fall in our spiritual senses, we are really free in our souls. But we must choose to live like we are free. We are free in our souls according to the law as Jesus met the whole law of Moses and sacrificed Himself that we might be properly positioned for a life of freedom—but if you are free and never activate your freedom through your soul and spiritual senses, are you really free? Freedom is ours but we must activate that freedom through our faith.

Jesus Recovered His Sight

You have most probably heard the story of the miracle of Jesus feeding 5,000 people with very little food. I would like to reveal some interesting insights concerning this story. Matthew 14:14-21 (NKJV) says:

> And when Jesus went out He ***saw*** a great multitude; and He was moved with compassion for them, and healed their sick. When it was evening, His disciples came to Him, saying, "This is a deserted place, and the hour is already late. Send the multitudes away, that they may go into the villages and buy themselves food." But Jesus said to them, "They do not need to go away. You give them something to eat." And they said to Him, "We have here only five loaves and two fish." He said, "Bring

> them here to Me." Then He commanded the multitudes to sit down on the grass. And He took the five loaves and the two fish, and ***looking up*** to heaven, He blessed and broke and gave the loaves to the disciples; and the disciples gave to the multitudes. So they all ate and were filled, and they took up twelve baskets full of the fragments that remained. Now those who had eaten were about five thousand men, besides women and children.

In this passage, the apostle Matthew tells us that Jesus saw the multitudes, and He had compassion on them. That word *multitude* in the Greek is *ochlos,* which means "a rabble, a special group of people"—broken down to the word *echo,* which reveals the class of people Jesus is talking about, meaning a possession or condition of diseased, fearful, full of lack, sick, having need. That's what Jesus saw when He looked at the people coming to hear Him speak.

Jesus told the disciples to give the people something to eat, but they only found five loaves of bread and two fish to offer more than 5,000 people. Even though Jesus saw the multitudes, He also saw the miracle to be done; *"looking up to heaven,"* He blessed the food and fed the people with an overflow of provision. The phrase *look up* or *looking up* in the Greek is *anablepo,* which means to "recover your sight."

We have the power to look up to Heaven and pray blessings, and God will take our act of faith and multiply what is in our hands to give to those in need of provision and healing.

This is a remarkable lesson in how to respond in life on a daily basis when talking about cracking the time code. When we look up to Heaven as our Source, we remember that all things have been redeemed and that God is our Source. He meets our faith when we choose to see with our spiritual eyesight by catapulting us into a spiritual place of abundancy, just like in the Garden of Eden. Looking up means we see God's goodness and love for us and for His people.

I have another remarkable thing from this Scripture I would like to share, and that is the fact that our Lord and Savior saw the multitude as in He looked down upon them. He saw from His holy position of *eido* covenant the diseased and those in need. The word *saw* in verse 14 is the word *eido*. It means Jesus was seeing from His spiritual covenant relationship with the Lord and He was witnessing their condition of depravity. It moved Him so much that He even had to reposition Himself to "recover His sight" as the word *anablepo* says. When Jesus had compassion, He moved from a place of spiritual sight to natural or earthly sight to see their depravity and sickness, and then He had to call Himself out of that place of depravity to do the miracle. This should encourage us.

If the Savior of the world can get overwhelmed by the depravity of humanity and the curse of the fall of man, then so can we. He had to *anablepo* in order to do the miracle and "recover His spiritual sight." To get back to His heavenly place of seeing as God sees, Jesus had to reposition Himself. How much more so will we have to do the same as we have sin in our DNA. We are redeemed from the curse because of what Jesus has done for us, and have been given access to the heavenlies. We need to keep this in mind because Jesus is our example and it is easy for us to get caught up in what we see around us in the world, and when we see too much depravity or sickness we can get swept up in it. We need to stop ourselves and *anablepo* or "recover our sight."

If that is you and you keep looking down, even seeing what needs to be fixed and you do not "recover your sight," you may get sucked right into it and the very thing you want to see happen with a miracle is not going to come to pass until you center yourself and look up or *anablepo* and "recover your sight"—then bless whatever that mess is, whatever those few loaves are, and watch God bring the overflow. Watch God bring the increase.

This is very important to know because every day we have a choice of *blepo* or *anablepo*, even from our *eido* covenant position that Jesus has given us as we are in Him. *Eido* and *anablepo* are two separate words, but very similar in meaning. When we read about the numerous miracles throughout the various parables, they were usually referring to the fact they were blind or *blepo* and then they saw *anablepo,* with their spiritual eyes.

People would say, "Jesus, I want my sight. Jesus, I want to see." And when Jesus did the miracle to open someone's eyes, it was usually referring to the fact they were blind or *blepo,* and then they saw *anablepo.*

Now you can live in the realms of the *anablepo* and *eido* all the time because Jesus did. How do I know that He did? It's as simple as reading Matthew 14:14-21 or Luke 9:12-17, because He had to recover His sight, which means that was His sight. If you must recover your sight, it means that was the original design or original way you were supposed to see. Jesus had to recover His sight because He lived there, and He tried to teach the disciples to live there, live in the fellowship, live in the relationship with the Father, live in this place of spiritual intimacy.

From *eido* and *anablepo,* you will be able to do signs, miracles, and wonders. I want you to live here and not here. But remember even Jesus in that moment took His eyes off of that place to see the depravity of the multitudes. We see the depravity in ourselves and humankind every day. We watch it, read about it in the news, and experience depravity daily. But thanks be to God, through Jesus Christ all things have been redeemed.

Now I must mention theologically that the fragmented pieces, the five loaves of bread and the two fish, all of that is symbolic of the broken body of Jesus and the multiplication of His "fish"—us. God does miracles when we look up and see that Jesus died, was buried, resurrected, and ascended to give us access to the heavenly places and eternal time so we can walk in the fullness of what has already been redeemed.

This type of redemption knowledge by faith opens portals from Heaven that release miracles on earth. When we choose to live as though all things are redeemed and we are in *eido* covenant with Father God because of Jesus's broken body and shed blood, then we are standing on who we are in Him and exercising the faith that will move mountains and shift atmospheres into abundancy. This move by Jesus to look up not only revealed that prosperity comes through His sacrifice, but that once we recognize that, increase and multiplication will begin to flow.

By faith we must first shift our focus to look up and live up there in the heavenly realms in our souls and our spirits. We must know that everywhere our body treads on earth and everywhere your feet tread, you'll take the land and miracles will be done—because the curse of the fall has been redeemed and time is now life, not death. We are now everlasting and everything is eternal. Your spirit and your soul must maintain the position of living with Him. It's a position of rest and peace and joy because peace and joy come from faith life realms, not death realms of lack and depravity.

Filled in the Garden of Eden

One last thing from this passage in Matthew 14:20 (KJV), which says, *"And they did all eat, and were filled: and they took up of the fragments that remained twelve baskets full."* This word *filled* is the Greek word *chortazo,* which means "to gorge as in a supply of food in abundance and to satisfy." This word is broken down to *chortos,* which means a court or garden, a pasture.

Now this is amazing. When Jesus *anablepo* and recovered His eyesight and God did the miracle through Him saying, "blessed" and He broke the bread, there was such an abundance of food it was like being in a garden. So when we *anablepo* and recover our sight, we can step into the heavenly realms; remember that the heavenly eternal realms are like the Garden of Eden. We again step into the redemption of the shed blood of Jesus Christ and the curse falls off and now we are living again in the abundancy of the Garden of Eden.

In this same Scripture passage it says, *"and they took up of the fragments that remained twelve baskets full."* That word *full* in the Greek is *pleres,* which means "to replete or cover over, to be complete." *Pleres* broken down is the word *pletho,* which means "to imbue, influence, supply, as in to fulfill time." Wow, this means when we *anablepo* and recover our sight in faith to live and believe that all things are redeemed because of what Jesus has done, then we catapult ourselves into a time code that is accomplished or complete. We live the endless life.

Remember Jesus had to do this too, yet He was the Savior of the universe, and how much more so do we now have access because He died, was buried, resurrected, and ascended. These verses in Matthew 14:14-21 and Luke 9:12-17 are the keys to learning to live back in the Garden of Eden, or as mentioned before is just like living in eternal time, nothing missing or broken, as though the fall of man never occurred. Jesus redeemed the time and all the resources that the curse of the fall robbed from us.

These Scriptures teach us a remarkable lesson in how to respond in life daily when talking about cracking the time code. When we look up to Heaven as our Source, we remember that all things have been redeemed and that God is our Source and He will come and meet our faith in our spiritual sight. This launches us into a spiritual place of abundancy, just like the garden of Eden.

It's a position where God has you and everything around you in His hands, even when you don't have control of you and everything around you.

Jesus relied on this level of knowledge. He relied on the fact that God had the situation under His control even when He wasn't sure whether or not He had it. Jesus knew He could look up to that heavenly place and faith would be activated. When He felt weak, His spiritual sight would open Him into the heavenly realms, the Garden of Eden experience where time is redeemed and the earth responds as such. Jesus instilled this revelatory faith in the disciples so they could do amazing miracles on earth and then pass that knowledge on to us.

We are living in that heavenly realm today. But when pressures come and difficulties happen and grief comes in along with sin and temptations and death and these kinds of depraved things, we can easily become wrapped up in this place of the curse of the fall that we forget who we are in Christ and we must *anablepo* or recover our sight, and live out being in *eido* covenant with the Lord.

The Two Gardens

I want to share with you some incredible parallels between the temptation of Adam and Eve that led to the curse of the fall of man and the temptation of the Garden of Gethsemane that Jesus went through. Jesus, when He was in the Garden of Gethsemane before going to the Cross, experienced the weight of living in an earthly realm, where we are under the power of the curse of the fall of man. Remember, He was Messiah, the One without sin. Yet He was tested in His flesh multiple times to qualify as our High Priest. The revelation of the two Gardens is incredibly important to understand what Jesus has done for us.

When we think of the process of redemption, our Savior Jesus Christ had to become our Passover Lamb and go through all that was necessary to break the curse. This breaking first began in the Garden of Gethsemane. That word *Gethsemane* means "oil press." This garden was a garden like the Garden of Eden and is even positioned near the actual Garden of Eden in Israel. They say the Garden of Eden was on Mount Moriah, which was near the Temple Mount in Jerusalem.

Adam, the first man, sinned in the Garden of Eden when tempted to eat of the tree of the Knowledge of Good and Evil by satan. But Jesus, the second Adam, suffered first in temptation in Gethsemane before going to the Cross. Here Jesus toiled in the Garden of Gethsemane with satan as he fought the temptation that faces all humankind. He asked the Lord three times for the cup to pass from Him that He may not have to die for the sins of the world (Matthew 26:36-46).

The three disciples whom Jesus brought with Him were so tempted themselves as they waited for Jesus in the Garden of Gethsemane that Jesus says in Matthew 26:41 (KJV), *"Watch and pray, lest you enter into temptation. The spirit indeed is willing, but the flesh is weak."* Their flesh wanted to sleep instead of pray for Jesus who was beginning His process of redeeming humanity.

Jesus redeemed the Garden of Eden through a process of first defeating temptation in the Garden of Gethsemane. He defeated this temptation even to the point of sweating blood (Luke 22:44). This type of agony is like the toiling we have from the curse of the fall of man. As He toiled, He was defeating the temptation, even in the Garden of Gethsemane, to run from His purpose and destiny. He was fighting as He felt the pain we experience as humans when we battle between the two realms of the earth and eternal. His agony and pain not only in the Garden of Gethsemane but, of course, on the Cross exemplifies His strength and obedience to submit to the Lord even unto death. Through this submission to God, He redeemed the curse and now we have the power to go through difficulties where we may want to say, "Lord, let this cup pass from me." We know we can persevere if we look up and remain steadfast against temptation.

Hebrews 2:17-18 (NKJV) says,

> Therefore, in all things He had to be made like His brethren, that He might be a merciful and faithful High Priest in things pertaining to God, to make propitiation for the sins of the people. For in that He Himself has suffered, being tempted, He is able to aid those who are tempted.

We, by our faith in what Jesus has done and as our example, can look up and see from where our help comes; it is from the Lord (Psalm 121:1). We are empowered now to seek God when we battle in our flesh and our eyes are on the ground instead of the heavenly realms. This is a real battle, but we can overcome if we keep our eyes fixed on Him.

In Matthew 11 is another example of the power of seeing and hearing correctly as though all things are redeemed. Remember, Jesus is the great Redeemer. By His shed blood we are all redeemed in humanity and so is our universe, which means time is redeemed.

Matthew 11:2-6 (NKJV) tells us:

> And when John had heard in prison about the works of Christ, he sent two of his disciples and said to Him, "Are You the Coming One, or do we look for another?" Jesus answered and said to them, "Go and tell John the

> things which you hear and see: The blind see and the lame walk; the lepers are cleansed and the deaf hear; the dead are raised up and the poor have the gospel preached to them. And blessed is he who is not offended because of Me."

Jesus responded to the two disciples who were sent to take back a message to John the Baptist and He said this, *"Go and tell John the things which you hear and see."* This word *hear* is the Greek word *akouo,* the word for natural hearing. The word *see* is the Greek word *blepo* for natural sight. Remember, natural sight is sight that is not yet redeemed, it is still in the curse of the fall.

But Jesus tells the disciples to make sure John knows signs and wonders are following His ministry and He says, *"The blind see and the lame walk; the lepers are cleansed and the deaf hear; the dead are raised up and the poor have the gospel preached to them."* This word *sight* is the word *anablepo,* which means people are "looking up" and their sight is recovering! It means that miracles are happening and they are being returned to their original condition as in the Garden of Eden with spiritual and natural sight returning.

Now here is an interesting discovery in the Greek, the same word *akouo* is used in both *hear* and *the deaf hear* in Matthew 11:4-5. Why? Because in this case Jesus is not speaking a parable, and no word is being administered, they are not becoming wiser, like *suniemi* hearing, so that is why *suniemi* is not used here in the Greek. They are only being healed in natural hearing. Whereas with the seeing, it is visual acuity as well as seeing spiritually that Jesus is the Son of God.

When we consider how Jesus was able to overcome under all temptation and pain, we can look to Hebrews 12:3-6 (NKJV) that reads:

> For consider Him who endured such hostility from sinners against Himself, lest you become weary and discouraged in your souls. You have not yet resisted to bloodshed, striving against sin. And you have forgotten the exhortation which speaks to you as to sons: "My son, do not despise the chastening of the Lord, nor be discouraged when you are rebuked by Him; for whom the Lord loves He chastens, and scourges every son whom He receives."

We will have times of despair or even discipline and chastisement. In all these times we can confidently say that if we keep our eyes on Him, He will carry us through.

Prayer of Faith

I want to pray for you right now. Maybe you are experiencing loss, depression, anxiousness, or overwhelmed with many things. You are only seeing things from an earthly perspective and it is hard to see from the heavenly or eternal. Let me encourage you, so did Jesus. But He looked up and looked to God no matter His circumstance. He is our High Priest in the order of Melchizedek and He has made a way for your healing now.

> *Lord, I am interceding for my friend right now. I ask that You help them look up in their times of distress and turn over in this earth realm everything that needs to be released. Please take them to the fullness of an eternal life. Take them to a place of seeing the end from the beginning so they can make right decisions and be catapulted into all You have for them. I thank You, Lord, that You are good and great and You love Your people—and those who humble themselves You will carry through*

the rough times in the earth realm. I thank You that You sent Your Son, Jesus, to redeem us from the curse of the fall of man and turn around the effects of the toil that we experience in this realm. Renew us and refresh us with a touch from the Holy Spirit. We love You and will believe in Your full redemption for our eternal life today.

10

The Miraculous and Prophetic in the New Eternal Order

God is the I AM and the I AM cracked the time code so that Heaven and earth could meet together and eternal time and earth time could sync for miracles to happen. This is part of the new eternal order. A key for miracles to happen is that the eyes of people must look up and submit to Heaven. There must be a receiving of faith and a tangible knowing in their souls that Jesus loves them and wants to indeed heal them. A faith that is a tangible in our souls where we know because of Jesus we can access what He did and we have the Holy Spirit within us. The Holy Spirit then comes and miracles occur.

I have seen many amazing miracles in my ministry. I'll share with you some of my experiences when I ministered in Finland. In September 2024 when I was there, the Lord had me prophesy healings and miracles and many were manifested. For example, a man who had breathing issues for 15 years and low oxygen levels. God worked a miracle for that man as he said he was refreshed during the prayer of faith and healing. God began to heal him by increasing his breathing capacity all night while he was sleeping.

A woman was healed who also had breathing issues. Her lungs were unhealthy for years; and in addition, she had tumbled down the stairs two times which caused chronic back pain and a disc injury. She had been in extreme pain for two to three years. God healed her and the pain was gone. With knees and elbows aching for years, she returned to the meeting the second day saying she was completely healed.

A woman was healed completely of dairy and lactose issues. She had asked God to heal her but she had forgotten about it. When I called out God was healing dairy issues, she knew it was for her, but she did not ask for God to heal her in that moment. Yet God reminded her she had prayed in the past for this healing. She thought in the natural, *Lord, people live with dairy and lactose issues, I do not need to get rid of lactose issues.* But she received the prophetic word and made it her own—then the power of God hit her and the next day she woke up and ate. She was healed in the name of Jesus.

Then in December 2024, again, this time through a faith activation I encouraged the people to "look up to heaven" and receive all the blessings God has already written for us. God brought many past things to people's minds. Even things they had packed away in their souls and were unsure would ever happen. In this meeting God opened a portal of remembrance to the people and they started remembering prayers. Then they began to receive what they had already asked God for but had not seen manifestation yet.

One of the ladies cupped her hands in the activation to receive blessings from Heaven when I said, "There is another level of healing gifts happening." She said, "I received that level, and I knew I was ready to go to the person God revealed to me to pray for healing."

One lady pictured in her mind as she looked up that she was doing creative miracles and when I said, "Another level of healing gifts is here," she came into agreement with receiving healing gifts at another level. She affirmed in her testimony that she believed and also knew exactly who she was to pray for now.

Faith Prayer and Activation

Maybe you have asked God for greater healing and creative miracle gifts; now is the time to receive. I feel faith is high at this moment and you are ready to receive. Just look up to Heaven and thank God for what He is giving you for this new season. I will do it with you!

> *Lord, we thank You and receive new levels of prophecy, healing, and miracles. New levels of spiritual gifts are coming forth for us. Thank You for removing any doubt and filling us to overflow as we look above and see what You want to give us both.*

We have had many lactose and digestive issues healed in our ministry. There was one young beautiful girl who wanted to eat/drink dairy products—cheese, milk, ice cream, butter, yogurt, etc. She and her lovely sister, who was much older, both had dairy issues, so their parents had to make them certain non-dairy foods to eat. During a healing service, they came to a new level of faith and asked that I pray for them to eat dairy. I did, and God met their faith and healed them both on the spot.

The faith levels were so high that evening after the service when I prayed, the little girl said to her mom, "I'm going to eat cheese." I saw the look on her mom's face, not sure she should do this, but the little girl's faith was so high. Sure enough, I was with them after the service, and she ate cheese. The next day she was fine. Then her sister tried it days later and realized that she was healed too. Now they both enjoy cheese and ice cream. They received in faith and they believed, and God did it! Believe God for your issues now and receive healing! Keep your faith high!

Jesus and His Miracles

The following are a few more instances of miracles that come from the redemption of time and how what Jesus did returns us to the original condition in the Garden of Eden or living from heavenly, eternal, ascension realms.

Matthew 20:29-34 (KJV) reads:

> And as they departed from Jericho, a great multitude followed him. And, behold, two blind men sitting by the way side, when they heard that Jesus passed by, cried out, saying, Have mercy on us, O Lord, thou son of David. And the multitude rebuked them, because they should hold their peace: but they cried the more, saying, Have mercy on us, O Lord, thou son of David. And Jesus stood still, and called them, and said, What will ye that I shall do unto you? They say unto him, Lord, that our eyes may be opened. So Jesus had compassion on them, and touched their eyes: and immediately their eyes received sight, and they followed him.

Another miracle was done as Jesus was moved by compassion, it says that He touched their eyes and they received sight. This word *sight* in verse 34 is *anablepo,* "to recover your sight." A side note, when Jesus touched their eyes, that word *touched* in the Greek is *hapto,* which means "to set on fire, or kindle a light." Pretty amazing how the fire of God will appear when we have compassion and faith to step out and believe.

Luke 18:35-43 (KJV) reads:

> And it came to pass, that as he was come nigh unto Jericho, a certain blind man sat by the way side begging: And hearing the multitude pass by, he asked what it meant. And they told him, that Jesus of Nazareth passeth by. And he cried, saying, Jesus, thou son of David, have mercy on me. And they which went before rebuked him, that he should hold his peace: but he cried so much the more, Thou son of David, have mercy on me. And Jesus stood, and commanded him to be brought unto him: and when he was come near, he asked him, Saying, What wilt thou that I shall do unto thee? And he said, Lord, that I may receive my ***sight***. And Jesus said unto him, Receive thy ***sight***: thy faith hath saved thee. And immediately he received his ***sight***, and followed him, glorifying God: and all the people, when they ***saw*** it, gave praise unto God.

In the last three verses, 41-43, the word *sight* is the Greek word *anablepo*. And then, *"when they saw it, gave praise unto God."* This word *saw* in the Greek is the word *eido,* the covenant word for those who have attached their faith, converted, and believe! This is the power to bring nonbelievers to faith in Jesus, when the unity of the believers are in *eido*.

This miracle happened because this blind man had faith to believe that Jesus could do a miracle for him. His faith was of the kind that put him back in the Garden of Eden to be made whole.

Think about this for a moment, if we want healing, we must believe all things are redeemed and made whole. This man believed his wholeness was coming through Jesus, but because of what Jesus did on the Cross, through His death, burial, resurrection, and ascension, technically all things have been redeemed so any miracles now are done out of the original design that God established for us. By faith we are catapulted back to the Garden of Eden; so by faith when we believe, we live there and can activate miracles. When you think on supernatural abundancy, you become supernaturally abundant. This supernatural abundance means you have faith, and the more revelation that comes from that faith, the more abundance will flow to you along with all its benefits.

The Kingdom of Heaven Mystery

Now regarding the benefits of faith and walking in the revelation and manifestation of the Kingdom of God, Jesus has this to say in Matthew 13:10-12 (NKJV):

> And the disciples came and said to Him, "Why do You speak to them in parables?" He answered and said to them, "Because it has been given to you to know the mysteries of the kingdom of heaven, but to them it has not been given. For whoever has, to him more will be given, and he will have abundance; but whoever does not have, even what he has will be taken away from him."

This means when we recognize our full redemption that Jesus bought us, we are at the beginning of the story. We are at the beginning of the original design for humankind in the Garden of Eden, to live in peace, joy, and abundancy in a world without sin or the curse of the fall and its effects. That is the beginning of the "mystery of the Kingdom of Heaven" and it is only for believers. If you have this beginning—you recognize your full redemption—you are open to more abundance. But if you don't even have initial salvation—you have not yet accepted Jesus as the Son of God and your personal Savior—you are shut out of the original blessing of redemption.

You are not shut out of healing, as God will heal you whether you are saved or not. But to live in a realm of faith for miracles is what we are talking about today, that is a different level of revelation. The original blessing includes full redemption of time and all resources—no lack and depravity—because death has been overcome and victorious living through the redemption that Jesus bought is ours.

That word *abundance* in the Greek is *perisseuo,* which means to "superabound in quantity and quality, to be in excess, to cause to make more, to excel and increase, to remain over and above."

This abundancy is ours who believe all things are redeemed and returned to the original design of the Garden of Eden, or as we have said definition-wise, to live in the heavenly realms seated with Christ in heavenly places of eternal everlasting life for the here and now. It also means "above and beyond that," which means once we grab hold of abundancy by faith, we are propelled into a new measure we can use for God's glory. Our original faith in Jesus—as being our Savior who redeemed everything back to us that Adam and Eve lost—now propels into a foundation that can produce increase in all aspects of life.

Everyone wants the increase but too many do not even have the foundation. The foundation is a basic place of belief for all in Jesus as our Redeemer and Savior. However, we must learn to go beyond this current level of faith and practice at another level as did the disciples, which is practice living here and operating in the effects beyond a foundation revelation of redemption. Redemption applies to a higher level of our soul (mind, will and emotions), living daily in the revelation of eternal time and full redemption of all.

This realm of faith living means everything you face in life daily has already been redeemed. It means looking through a daily lens or filter into the world around you and responding like you are in the Garden of Eden, even when there is no evidence you can see. It means everything you are faced with must come into agreement with what Jesus already did and how He put us back into the Garden of Eden, which, as the apostle Paul says, seats us with Christ in heavenly places (Ephesians 2:6). This is living as the apostle Paul says, *"be not conformed to this world: but be ye transformed by the renewing of your mind, that ye may prove what is that good, and acceptable, and perfect, will of God"* (Romans 12:2 KJV).

Again, this seating on Jesus's lap is where our High Priest intercedes daily for us and where the new eternal order of Melchizedek plays out daily. All things are redeemed under the eternal order, which means now we don't fear when it appears we are in lack on earth—now we stand for the new and living way made manifest. From this place of faith, we activate the abundancy needed to refute the lack we are surrounded with daily. The enemy loses his power when we have such faith, which opens the door to greater abundancy and greater miracles and greater effects of what we have received.

Matthew 10:7-8 (KJV) Jesus says, *"And as ye go, preach, saying, The kingdom of heaven is at hand. Heal the sick, cleanse the lepers, raise the dead, cast out devils: freely ye have received, freely give."*

Jesus says in Him is the Kingdom of Heaven that arrived when He walked the earth. How much more so is the Kingdom now that He died, was buried, resurrected, ascended, and fulfilled the earthly requirements of the law and sacrifice as our High Priest.

In earth time, all requirements are now met and the new eternal order of Melchizedek has now arrived. We have freely received a new eternal order, and from this place of abundancy we now do miracles that cause us to live out being Jesus's disciples.

Saul's Revelation

The key to the *more than* experience is the initial experience, then after you have initial salvation, your soul must practice realizing that all things are returned to you in the Garden of Eden. You must practice knowing that the vats of Heaven as yours. Remember, the Garden of Eden is like the heavenly places with all the vats of grain, wine, oil (Hosea 2, Joel 2). These are all yours.

We must operate knowing that nothing is missing or broken; this is the new eternal order. This revelation and wisdom in our souls changes everything—now we have truly received and our souls are full to overflowing; we have entered eternal time and resources, there is no more lack; by faith and revelation, we walk in miracles, signs and wonders, heal the sick, cleanse the leper, raise the dead, and cast out devils.

The great apostle Paul also received his sight when he was touched. Acts 9:1-22 (NKJV) tells us:

> Then Saul, still breathing threats and murder against the disciples of the Lord, went to the high priest and asked letters from him to the synagogues of Damascus, so that if he found any who were of the Way, whether men or women, he might bring them bound to Jerusalem.
>
> As he journeyed he came near Damascus, and suddenly a light shone around him from heaven. Then he fell to the ground, and heard a voice saying to him, "Saul, Saul, why are you persecuting Me?"

And he said, "Who are You, Lord?"

Then the Lord said, "I am Jesus, whom you are persecuting. It is hard for you to kick against the goads." So he, trembling and astonished, said, "Lord, what do You want me to do?" Then the Lord said to him, "Arise and go into the city, and you will be told what you must do."

And the men who journeyed with him stood speechless, hearing a voice but seeing no one. Then Saul arose from the ground, and when his eyes were opened he saw no one. But they led him by the hand and brought him into Damascus. And he was three days without sight, and neither ate nor drank.

Now there was a certain disciple at Damascus named Ananias; and to him the Lord said in a vision, "Ananias." And he said, "Here I am, Lord." So the Lord said to him, "Arise and go to the street called Straight, and inquire at the house of Judas for one called Saul of Tarsus, for behold, he is praying. And in a vision he has seen a man named Ananias coming in and putting his hand on him, so that he might receive his sight."

Then Ananias answered, "Lord, I have heard from many about this man, how much harm he has done to Your saints in Jerusalem. And here he has authority from the chief priests to bind all who call on Your name."

But the Lord said to him, "Go, for he is a chosen vessel of Mine to bear My name before Gentiles, kings, and the children of Israel. For I will show him how many things he must suffer for My name's sake."

And Ananias went his way and entered the house; and laying his hands on him he said, "Brother Saul, the Lord Jesus, who appeared to you on the road as you came, has sent me that you may receive your sight and

> be filled with the Holy Spirit." Immediately there fell from his eyes something like scales, and he received his sight at once; and he arose and was baptized.
>
> So when he had received food, he was strengthened. Then Saul spent some days with the disciples at Damascus. Immediately he preached the Christ in the synagogues, that He is the Son of God. Then all who heard were amazed, and said, "Is this not he who destroyed those who called on this name in Jerusalem, and has come here for that purpose, so that he might bring them bound to the chief priests?"
>
> But Saul increased all the more in strength, and confounded the Jews who dwelt in Damascus, proving that this Jesus is the Christ.

Saul became Paul and went from *blepo* to *anablepo*. He recovered His sight and then began to preach the gospel immediately. The recovery of our sight is the beginning of being able to carry the spiritual gifts God has for us. Your gift will be used mightily when you can practice your gifting from a place of faith in the full redemption of the revelation of the Garden of Eden, eternal realms. In the new eternal order of Melchizedek, our gifts can flow freely and without hindrance because we believe Jesus redeemed all things.

Kingdom Eyes Opened

Ephesians 4:11-16 (KJV) reads:

> And he gave some, apostles; and some, prophets; and some, evangelists; and some, pastors and teachers; For the ***perfecting*** of the saints, for the work of the ministry, for the edifying of the body of Christ: Till we all come in

> the unity of the faith, and of the knowledge of the Son of God, unto a perfect man, unto the measure of the stature of the fulness of Christ: That we henceforth be no more children, tossed to and fro, and carried about with every wind of doctrine, by the sleight of men, and cunning craftiness, whereby they lie in wait to deceive; but speaking the truth in love, may grow up into him in all things, which is the head, even Christ: From whom the whole body fitly joined together and compacted by that which every joint supplieth, according to the effectual working in the measure of every part, maketh increase of the body unto the edifying of itself in love.

Our responsibility as the church is to now step into the new and living way so we can bring the Kingdom of Heaven to earth and renew it knowing that the Garden of Eden has been redeemed. This fullness that we are moving into has nothing missing or broken, just like Heaven. The whole reason for the spiritual gifts is to fix what is broken and perfect the saints. That word *perfecting* in Ephesians 4 in the Greek is *katartismos,* which means "complete furnishing" and is broken down to the word *katartizo,* which means to repair or restore, to make complete and thorough, as in to mend or adjust.

Through the death, burial, resurrection, and ascension of Jesus Christ, we, His church, are seated with Him in heavenly places:

> But unto every one of us is given grace according to the measure of the gift of Christ. Wherefore he saith, When he ascended up on high, he led captivity captive, and gave gifts unto men. (Now that he ascended, what is it but that he also descended first into the lower parts

> of the earth? He that descended is the same also that ascended up far above all heavens, that he might fill all things.) (Ephesians 4:7-10 KJV)

Jesus ascended and put His blood on the mercy seat to fulfill the requirements of the mosaic law so that He could give us gifts to fix the church. Now He has ascended permanently, and the church is ascended with Him. We are now with Him in this place, and by faith all the benefits of His redemption on earth are made evident in Heaven and earth by those who believe and dare to walk it out. We must be the ones who see beyond our natural sight and see from our spiritual *anablepo* sight, having the ability to "recover our sight" daily so we can live out the new eternal order of Melchizedek by believing in the Garden of Eden redemption. When we do this and live here in our souls, all aspects of life will flourish and abundancy will come as we exercise our gifts and see signs, miracles, and wonders.

From this place the glory of God is released on earth. We must believe in the new and living way completely bought for us by Jesus. We must share this truth and walk it out in unity with the church before we will see it made manifest fully on earth. Remember, it has all been redeemed and the time code has been cracked. But can we walk it out, like it is really finished? Yes! When we do He is made manifest through our faith in His redemption and the gifts flow from here.

Kingdom Manifestation

I urge the church to live in this level of faith of what was redeemed by Christ and all things will change forevermore. If the Kingdom is so confounded and confused and unsure of its identity, it won't be able to stand in the places that Jesus already redeemed for us. It's not that it hasn't already been done, it's how do we apply it? How do we make it work? And so this is our test every day. Our test: are we going to stand in the Kingdom, declare the victory, live in the places of rest and peace and wholeness and holiness and purity and righteousness, declaring and decreeing what is right and true and good and merciful? Are we declaring what Jesus did on earth to redeem time, which means to give us back our eternal life?

Or, are we going to shrink back and become overwhelmed with the tsunami of darkness that is simply lying to us on an everyday basis? Yes, lying. The enemy is daily telling us that all things are not redeemed and now is the time to freak out over provision, protection, and acceptance. The enemy only has power when we don't live by faith like all things are redeemed. We must believe this and tell him the curse was broken. We must realize that we have access to everlasting life and its abundancy on earth today because of Jesus.

These are choices we must make.

When the Kingdom can hold one another accountable, and nations hold one another accountable to stand for the Kingdom, we can shift ourselves into living in that place. In my book *365 Prophetic Revelations from the Hebrew Calendar,* you can learn prophetically the time and seasons and how important it is for us to be already living out Kingdom redemption today. I teach you about the revelation of the ages and we have a small number of years before we enter the year 6,000, considered to be a new age. (Not the "New Age" counterfeit God.) I mean a new age according to Scripture. Scripture ages are based on 1,000 years or 2,000 years. We're going to step into a new age called the 6,000 point. Every 500 years prior to a new age is what's called transition. So we are in a transitionary movement that all of the cultures of earth are going through. This means that all of us today are born to be a transitionary prophet.

That doesn't mean you're called to the office of prophet. It means we are the people of God. And so the voice of prophecy is a way we declare and decree the voice of God on earth. The voice of prophecy is our testifying about Jesus. God calls us a prophetic people. We are called to prepare the way of the Lord, just like John the Baptist. And more now than ever because we're approaching the Kingdom age of 6,000. We won't see it, our kids won't see it, our great-grandchildren *will* see it. But what we teach today's youth makes all the difference. We must teach our children and our children's children the revelation that they are transitioning the entire earth to the return of the King.

There are specific things that must take place during these transitionary times. And one of those is the Kingdom physically arising and taking its proper position. We are being challenged by God in these end times to step up and be who we really are. He's saying stop talking *about* who you are and start *being* who you are.

God says, "You're talking a lot and you're putting the gospel out there and that's a good thing, but I need you to physically be in this game. I need you to physically link arms. I need you to physically say no to certain things. I need you to physically stand up. I need you to get involved in places that you have shunned. I need you to physically do what you need to do to make the difference as a righteous member of My Kingdom because I'm coming back. But I am not coming back for a world in disarray. I'm coming back for a world that lives like all things have been redeemed and are under the everlasting power of life, which means they have cracked the time code and death does not hinder time. They know they have the power of an endless life and a new eternal order that was established and they have to implement this on earth." That's what I believe God is saying to us.

I know many been taught that Jesus is going to show up and fix it all. But He already fixed it more than 2,000 years ago, that's what I read in the Bible, God's Word. I read that it's been done and redeemed. I read it's been finished and we live in a new eternal order where time has been redeemed and it is the power that we now carry. And because the power of what's been finished has been given to me and to my family and to the generations behind me, my job is to stand up and say it's finished. He said it's finished. So that's my job and your job. And if we don't do that, then we are failing. I do not want to fail because I'm fearful or shrink back because a demon seems bigger than me—the demons of media and government or any of the "seven mountains" (business, government, media, arts/entertainment, education, family, religion) that look too big to tackle. The Lord says, "Don't shrink back from taking hold of what I've already done because that means you don't believe Me."

It means we don't believe enough in what He's already done, which means we have to go back to the beginning and find out what He did exactly and how that empowers us to keep moving. Go back, yes to salvation as a foundation and then how His Kingdom is built on what His shed blood accomplished. Because it's been accomplished, our job prophetically—we are transitionary prophets—it to walk out what Jesus already did. And when we do, everywhere we tread in full redemption of what Jesus did!

The environment has to change to being fully redeemed, which means life must flow. It's not questionable. It's not like, well, maybe it might change. No, where's your faith? It will change. Why? Because you're there and because you've recovered your sight and because you're living in the Garden and you're in the place of rest that has been completed. The curse has been broken. Now you can speak life.

If we don't take hold of this new and living way of life, who will? We get angry seeing crazy people doing nutty stuff today and getting away with it. We say, "Why don't they change? Why aren't they respectful and have any common sense?" Do you really expect them to change if we don't even make an effort to change our way of thinking and living? We are the sons and daughters of the King. They won't change until we stand up as examples. When they see something different in us—the Holy Spirit—they will feel a conviction of sin and begin to see differently. A repentance will fall upon them and they may come to know the knowledge of Jesus as their Lord and Savior, just as mentioned at the beginning of the chapter when we talked about *blepo* sight and *eido* sight that comes at salvation.

You are more than you see yourself to be. The work is done. Do not be afraid of people. The enemy throws fear, but faith overrules all fear. And who do we believe in? We believe in the One who finished the work, the mighty Son of God, Jesus.

Isaiah 43:18-19 (NIV) says, *"Forget the former things; do not dwell on the past. See, I am doing a new thing! Now it springs up; do you not perceive it? I am making a way in the wilderness and streams in the wasteland."*

You may feel as if you are living in a wilderness, a wasteland, but God is doing a *new thing*. Can we, the people of God, not perceive something new is happening? Let's always remember that we are above, not beneath. We are the head, not the tail. We have God's favor. We're blessed to be a blessing!

Isaiah 65:8 (NKJV), *"Thus says the Lord: 'As the new wine is found in the cluster, and one says, "Do not destroy it, for a blessing is in it," so will I do for My servants' sake, that I may not destroy them all.'"* We are a cluster of new wine in the new eternal order of Melchizedek when we come together as one body in unity and use our gifts in this new eternal order.

Faith Activation

I want you to look up to Heaven right now. God spoke to the apostle John saying in Revelation 4:1-2 (NKJV):

> After these things I ***looked***, and behold, a door standing open in heaven. And the first voice which I heard was like a trumpet speaking with me, saying, "Come up here, and I will show you things which must take place after this." Immediately I was in the Spirit; and behold, a throne set in heaven, and One sat on the throne.

That word *looked* in the Greek is *eido*. God was calling apostle John to identify with His covenant with him and come up to eternal time and live here while John was on the island of Patmos in a place of rest and peace and with spiritual sight and cracking the time code right where he was.

Let us "look up" to our proper covenant position with Jesus as His church body.

> *Father, we receive from Heaven right now an impartation to have our spirit sight shifted from blepo to anablepo and eido covenant. I thank You, Father, that as we begin to see and hear with heavenly ears and not earthly ears, with heavenly eyes and not earthly eyes, we will begin to manifest the Kingdom everywhere we go. We thank You, Father, that everywhere our feet tread that you are fully redeeming the time and we are being properly positioned to rule on earth.*

Supernaturally, I feel that fire in the name of Jesus. Maybe your hands seem to be on fire right now. If so, that's a fire of impartation coming from Heaven. That's the fire of His Word.

When His Word goes out, fire comes to affirm. He is touching your spirit. He's touching your soul and switching your eyes to see spiritually. If you have vision problems in the natural, I believe that once spiritual sight hits you, your natural sight will change. It's going to shift in the mighty name of Jesus.

> *Lord, I thank You right now for healing someone's hearing. Lord, I ask for fire to open ears. Lord, I thank You for changing natural hearing to hearing the secret things in Your Kingdom, a hearing of the angels, a hearing of trumpets, a hearing of the prophetic word. Lord, I thank You for a new and fresh hearing to this prophetic person reading this right now. Lord, I thank You for the prophetic, transitionary prophets who need to hear Your Word. They need to hear what You're saying. They need to hear You every moment, Lord, that it might be made manifest through their mouths and their actions on earth right now.*

In the name of Jesus, I speak over you a new voice right now—new voice, new sound, not only in your ears but coming out of your mouth. In the mighty name of Jesus there's going to be a shift and all of a sudden you won't even understand, but what you're hearing will be so heavenly with such wisdom, such revelation, such knowledge. It will then come out of your mouth in the name of Yeshua and everywhere your mouth goes, fire will come forth and the angels of fire will come in alignment with your mouth and every voice, every spark, fire, and thunder represents the voice of God.

Impartation for Prophetic Ministry

You may be in heavy intercession for others on a continual level; you've been praying and been prophesying what's to come—

and in that prophetic, God is getting ready to give you a promotion to stand in a different seat.

I thank You, Father, for this impartation of the prophetic in the new age as the new age is approaching right now today. Lord, I thank You right now that young prophets are going to be given a microphone and they will stand in ways that they have not stood before. This is not just about giving a "good dessert" word to draw people into the gospel. This is about the seriousness of the prophetic. This is about being able to speak prophetically in a way that will not only convict, but will also bring life.

Father, I thank You for this prophet you're calling forth and who will prophesy from Heaven first. Who is not prophesying from earth to Heaven, but from Heaven to earth.

Activation of Mantles

Lord, I thank You for this reader who is looking up and seeing the powerful move that's happening. Let God touch you. He's calling you to speak up for His Kingdom, to move into another level of prophecy that isn't just taking the microphone to have people notice you. I rip that attitude off you in the name of Jesus. May you not carry an agenda. May you not have your own motive. May you not try and impress people. Prophecy is not about any of that. Humble yourself right now. This is about purity. This is about holiness. This is about righteousness.

You're going to stand before people and declare and decree what the Lord has said. This is no joke. You're going to reveal to the lost and lonely tonight, tomorrow, over the next weeks, and months everything they need to know about their heavenly Father, in the mighty name of Jesus.

But you can't wear the mantle if you can't let some stuff go. You probably know what I'm talking about. Thank You, Lord, for giving Your children the confidence to walk in the shed blood of Jesus Christ. Thank You, Jesus. My prayer for you is that you don't try to impress anyone except your heavenly Father. He wants authenticity. He doesn't want eloquent words. He doesn't want all that fluff stuff. He wants to say what people need to know through you. You are a vessel. A broken one. That's what you are.

In this new eternal order, you may be a prophet who is moving on to an apostolic calling, or you carry both gifts. You may be going on to some new opportunities as God has called for a prophetic and apostolic release right now and opportunities are going to come quickly. You may be called to sing a new song of creativity at a new level. That's part of prophecy too. Singing, writing. You may excel and stand out exceptionally in various areas of ministry. And you may receive financial blessings to advance the gifting that God has given you, but not because of a gift, but because He has something He wants to say to the world through you. Your resources are given to you to advance His Kingdom.

Lord, we thank You as we receive this impartation of your wisdom, your revelation. We thank You for the Kingdom arising. We thank You for setting us apart.

Also, I pray for spiritual sight to come on you in dreams and visions. You're going to encounter the supernatural. You're going to awake with testimonies to share that will touch people's hearts and spirits. You're going to have fire. Supernatural fire will hit you in the middle of the night. You will have angel-of-fire moments. God will be purifying your flesh. Lord, we give you glory, honor, and praise. Lord, we thank You. Continue to touch us throughout the nights and bring us fresh revelation in the mornings.

I hear the Lord saying, "Some of My children are being called out to write the Good News of Jesus Christ. Some believers have books to bring forth to advance My Kingdom." The Lord wants you to start writing. Get out your pen, power up your laptop. Even tonight, He may wake you up. You need to write some revelation now. What you have been asking for, God is going to bust open Heaven and release it. Prophetic people need to learn how to write about and for His glory.

I thank You, Father God, for what You did in this chapter. Lord Jesus, we ask that you continue to minister to us so that we become the Kingdom arising together.

Amen!

11

Eternal Riches Are Yours

I want to tell you a story about eternal riches that happened to me when I was in Washington, DC, to attend the Christian Inaugural Ball for President's Trump inauguration on January 20, 2025.

It was one of the coldest days in Washington, DC, and all of the festivities I was invited to were being held downtown at the Westin Hotel—in the perimeter that was blocked off. It was a crazy time as I had to arrive in the city early for my friends and me to register for the ball. The hotel where I booked a room was blocks away, and it was snowing. Even though we arrived early, we couldn't make it to the Westin without parking far away and Ubering the rest of the way. The ball was that night, and we didn't have enough time after we registered for the ball to return to our booked hotel room.

I was in line at the Westin registration desk asking questions when a kind man said, "I have an extra room in this hotel, who wants it?" My friend and I immediately raised our hands. "Yes, we want it!"

We were given a beautiful paid-for room in the Westin for our entire time in DC; and although our car was parked down the street because the Westin was in the safety perimeter, we were close enough to have time to walk to get our luggage, return to the hotel, and get changed for the event.

We praised God immensely; He provided what we needed at the right time. We went to the ball and it was beautiful; we had a wonderful time. There was assigned seating and at our table were some lovely folks we met for the first time. The lady shared with us that she had traveled a far distance by herself from Florida and was staying with a friend who was not in attendance at the ball. She lived quite a distance away and could only get into the city for the inaugural events by train.

I had asked the Lord about who to give our other hotel room to and the Lord told me in that moment, "She's the lady, give it to her." So we told her our story and how God provided a room in this very hotel for us—and that we had an extra room paid for just down the street if she wanted it. She was ecstatic! She was so happy and we were so happy to bless her. God had the time code cracked already. He knew we'd be running late and would need a room in this hotel, and He knew we would be seated with this woman, and He knew that this woman and her friend needed our other hotel room. It was awesome to see eternal riches ordained for us come to pass in the moment. We were all living in a realm of supernatural provision ready to give, and give abundantly, and God provided a culture of Heaven for us. This was a *kairos* moment made manifest in *chronos* time.

Cinderella Makes the Ball

The other amazing thing, prior to all of this happening on January 20, was I had a dream on January 1 that I was Cinderella and

I was looking for special shoes and I was trying not to be late to the ball. Mmm...sounds like God was preparing me before it even happened. I found out a week later that we received special tickets to the inaugural events. God gave us desires to go to where He was calling us in the eternal realms and then we walked it out in the earth realms by faith.

Maybe you have similar stories? Perhaps God spoke to you through dreams, visions, a prophetic word—and then it happened. The dream and prophecy was a revelation of the future that God wanted to make happen in the present. It was eternal time revelation coming to pass in the earth time zone. This is how it works.

A good friend and his wife asked me to pray for them when I was leaving a service. I saw in the spirit realms, eternal realms, that this young man was going to be on a television show and have his own show. I told him this. He laughed and said he didn't know anything about this. Then a few weeks later, he was invited to host his own show—which is now seen worldwide. He told me that if I had not prophesied that to him, when he was offered the opportunity *(kairos* moment in earth time), he may have passed it up. But because God said it, he was able to receive it when it was offered to him.

Eternity knows the plans God has for you in earth time. I am not sharing these stories to share about me or my prophetic gifts. The stories are to glorify God and to inform you about how He talks to us to prepare us. Remember Ecclesiastes 3:11 (NIV): *"He has made everything beautiful in its time. He has also set eternity in the human heart; yet no one can fathom what God has done from beginning to end."* We have to have the world in our hearts revealed and brought to light so *He can make everything beautiful in His time.*

True Riches Are Eternal First

In this chapter we learn about accessing the true riches of Heaven in eternal time. Because Jesus cracked the time code, we can now walk in the eternal wealth and riches of the Kingdom as though we are in the Garden of Eden. I'm excited to share with you straight from Scripture some revelation, wisdom, and knowledge that we need to have to understand how to walk in these heavenly realms and receive blessings from those places. Because the earth time code has been cracked and we are now living in the eternal realms by faith, we can position ourselves as receivers of the eternal blessings of God. Our mindsets must shift to asking, "How can I receive what God has already ordained for me to have?" I don't know about you, but that sounds like a restful place to me.

We are spending way too much time trying to figure out how we can get the biggest gain in our life. What I mean by gain is that our human DNA is programmed from the curse of the fall of man to always gain something. Our every thought is how we can gain provision, protection, and acceptance because those are the three things we lost in the curse of the fall. We are constantly thinking, *What's the next gain in my life? I'm going to work for this gain or work for that gain.* It's one thing to have creative ideas come from Heaven where God wants to use you in a mighty way to be a huge blessing to humanity. But it's another thing to work hard only to selfishly gain things that don't really matter.

As mentioned in previous chapters, working is overwhelming and ineffective when you are working from the curse of the fall. That is toiling to gain. You don't want to work from the stronghold of the fall, instead you want to work from the freedom that we have in Christ. It's a different way.

I love to work. I love to fulfill the purpose and destiny that God has placed on my life, but I don't want to do it without a fellowship relationship with the Lord, without being in that special place of peace and joy with Him—because that's really what life is all about, walking with Him in the cool of the day in the Garden of the Eden.

The Rich Young Ruler

Jesus made a way for that to happen for us when He died, was buried, resurrected, ascended, and broke the earth time code to return the riches and wealth of the eternal time zone. We are going to see how that works today when it comes to wealth building. There are many parables where Jesus speaks about wealth and riches. Why does Jesus spend time on this topic? Because He's teaching a Kingdom principle through earthly understanding. From that earthly understanding, He then kicks us into a new revelation of what God's Kingdom is all about.

Jesus is a master Teacher. In Luke 18, we're going to read about the wealthy ruler. There are different interpretations of this Scripture, and I teach from the standpoint that Jesus Himself knew about the wealth of the Kingdom. He knew about the treasuries and vats in Heaven that would be released in the glory for those who believed in Him as Lord and Savior. If we are willing to step in by faith to the realms of the ascension, these faith realms where all we receive is by His goodness, love, and grace, then we are ready for true riches. In this passage, we find that there was a certain rich young ruler, and the dialogue between him and Jesus goes like this.

Luke 18:18-27 (NKJV) reads:

> Now a certain ruler asked Him, saying, "Good Teacher, what shall I do to inherit eternal life?" So Jesus said to him, "Why do you call Me good? No one is good but One, that is, God. You know the commandments: 'Do not commit adultery,' 'Do not murder,' 'Do not steal,'

> 'Do not bear false witness,' 'Honor your father and your mother.'" And he said, "All these things I have kept from my youth." So when Jesus heard these things, He said to him, "You still lack one thing. Sell all that you have and distribute to the poor, and you will have treasure in heaven; and come, follow Me." But when he heard this, he became very sorrowful, for he was very rich. And when Jesus saw that he became very sorrowful, He said, "How hard it is for those who have riches to enter the kingdom of God! For it is easier for a camel to go through the eye of a needle than for a rich man to enter the kingdom of God." And those who heard it said, "Who then can be saved?" But He said, "The things which are impossible with men are possible with God."

Now here we go again, talking about eternity. This rich young ruler wants to know how to get to the realms of eternity. This young man is thinking, *Jesus, You're walking the earth. You're Messiah, You are my Savior. And if I believe in You, I want to know how I can access eternal life and all the blessings that are involved with that.*

Access Eternal Riches

When we access eternal life, we access all of the prosperity of the eternal. How do I know that? Because the culture of Heaven is no buying and selling, everything is full of giving and it is righteousness, peace, and joy. His Kingdom is filled with blessings. And so here we have this wealthy young ruler asking, "What can I do to inherit eternal life?" And Jesus says, *"Why do you call Me good? No one is good but One, that is God."* In other words, Jesus is pointing to the importance of nothing being good, even riches. Only God Himself is good. And so the young man says, in essence, "Listen, Jesus, I know all the commandments. I don't commit adultery, don't kill, don't steal. I don't bear false witness. I honor my mother and father. And, Master, I have kept all of these from my youth."

And when Jesus heard these things, He says to him (paraphrased), "Alright, that's great, rich young ruler, but you lack one thing. Sell all that you have and distribute the money to the poor and then you'll have treasure in Heaven, then come follow Me."

Giving Is the Heart of Heaven

There's nothing wrong with being rich on earth. This rich young ruler was probably a really great guy, a good young man, and he was very, very excited about inheriting eternal life and following Jesus. He had kept the commandments. He was a good Jew. He had done what he was supposed to be doing according to the Torah, and Jesus was not condemning any of that, not even his earthly riches.

Jesus was giving the man a glimpse of what it's like to live in Heaven. Jesus in essence was saying, "When you believe in Me and inherit eternal life, you are going to receive much more than you have here on earth." Jesus was shifting this parable and saying, "Listen, rich young ruler, I'm going to give you some advice here. If you want eternal life and you want to live forever with Me in the Kingdom, I want you to start now by knowing first that there isn't any buying and selling going on in eternal life or the heavenly realms. So, get rid of everything including your current thought processes. Get rid of the gain mindset and step into the real treasures found only in Heaven." Jesus is saying, "Young man, you asked Me about eternal life. Well, let me tell you what's in eternity for you."

Jesus was setting the stage for what eternity is like, and how we should be operating here on earth. He was explaining what life looks like with the earth time code being interrupted and the eternal time code of wealth and blessing of the Kingdom being administered. Jesus was explaining what Heaven is like. Not only is time extended as there is no beginning and no end, there's no lack, there's no death, there's no loss—there's more than enough. It is limitless.

Everything is filled to capacity and overflowing and, in essence, Jesus is saying, "If you believe in Me by faith, sow everything you have here on the earth and come follow Me and you will inherit treasure from Heaven *now*." In other words, Jesus was saying there exists in a realm of faith here on earth—because the time code is broken and all things are redeemed by faith—that you can have all your heavenly treasure now if only you believe in Him. Jesus is saying, "I am the Messiah who has come to crack the time code."

This revelation is powerful. God is speaking to you right now and the Lord's saying to you, "I want you to tap into My heavenly resources that come from inheriting eternal life, and all the blessings of eternal time, where nothing is missing or broken any longer." When we inherit eternal life by confessing Jesus as our Lord and Savior, it means we will live forever and gain Heaven in the here and now, in this time and space of earth.

From the moment we receive Jesus as our Lord and Savior, we also gain everything that exists in its fullness in eternal realms by faith—and if we learn to walk out on earth living from that place now, then Jesus affirms we are living by faith. This is why He challenged the rich young ruler because He knew the rich young ruler had put a lot into his earthly possessions and into his gain, but Jesus was inviting him to go to a new place in faith where he would have more than he had in the earth realms.

Do you want more than you have now in the earth realms? The young ruler was rich. He didn't need any more here, yet he never heard anyone say, "Sell it all and be with nothing and then you'll tap in to the greatness of My eternal Kingdom." I'm excited about this because Jesus is offering heavenly riches to this rich young ruler who supposedly had more than enough, then his message is pertinent to us who think we don't have enough, right? Jesus is saying, "Listen, it's time for Me to take you to the wealthy places." I don't know about you, but I want to go to those wealthy places. I know the Word of God and I know who God is to get there by faith.

Wealthy Realms

Now let's shift your mind to go to that place of living in the wealthy realms. When we talk about wealth, it's a wholeness word. It means nothing missing and nothing broken. It's a shalom word or a prosperous word. It doesn't just mean what's the pocket change in your hand? What's the gold and silver you have at your disposal? Living in a wealthy place means living in the culture of Heaven, the ascension realms, having that manifestation of a life of fullness and prosperity in every way.

Jesus is teaching the rich young ruler by using what was dear to the young man, which was his riches and all of his possessions, to bring this revelation home. In Luke 18:18-27, the young rich ruler asked, *"What shall I do to inherit eternal life?"* He was really asking, "How do I get to the place that's more than enough, not just what I see in my hands?"

The young ruler's heart was saying, "Jesus, I know one day I'm going to die and I don't know where all this is going to go. I want to be in that place, the place that's more than enough."

Even a rich man recognizes the fact that what he has wasn't enough to sustain him. That there is another life accessible to him if he believes in Jesus as Messiah.

When you believe in Jesus as Messiah, you get the full benefits of the wealth and currency of Heaven in the here and now.

That's exactly what Jesus is telling the young man saying, "You're asking for eternal life, but I'm giving you a principle right now that can activate access to true riches now, in this moment. Go and sell everything you have if you believe in Me. Young man, I am offering you a faith challenge that will bring the true riches you have been waiting for. You have been stewarding earthly riches, you are ready for heavenly ones—but they only come by knowing Me and having faith in the release of heavenly riches now. I am the Messiah who can give you this access." You probably know what the Scriptures say happened to the young man.

Luke 18:23-25 (NKJV) says:

> But when he heard this, he became very sorrowful, for he was very rich. And when Jesus saw that he became very sorrowful, He said, "How hard it is for those who have riches to enter the kingdom of God! For it is easier for a camel to go through the eye of a needle than for a rich man to enter the kingdom of God."

Jesus wasn't saying rich people are having difficulty getting into the Kingdom of God. That's not what He's saying. You can be very rich and enter the Kingdom of God. As a matter of fact, your riches are a huge benefit to the earth realm. You just need to be a distributor of those resources. It is a blessing to be wealthy on earth. There's so much that God can speak to you about with the provision that you have so you can be a blessing to the Kingdom of Heaven on earth today.

Treasuries in Heaven

This parable wasn't directed at whether you're rich or poor. God just knew where the heart of this young ruler was. He wanted to do the right thing, but the young man had put so much time and effort into the gain that he had on earth that he found his identity stewarding this earthly wealth.

When he was sorrowful, Jesus said to him, in essence, "It's hard for those who are rich to enter the Kingdom of God because it is a greater act of faith for you to believe Me, than someone who has little. And it may be even harder for you to believe when I die, shed My blood for you, am buried, and I resurrect and you resurrect with Me, and sin, death in the grave is broken, and then I ascend—but you get way more than what's currently in your hand."

Jesus was inviting the rich young ruler to know the secrets of the cracked time code, to be a steward now on earth by faith and learn to steward the resources of Heaven now even before the young man's death when his body goes into the ground and his spirit and soul go to Heaven. Jesus was challenging his faith, to believe more in the eternal realms and how they affect the earth realms now, as the *"kingdom of heaven is at hand"* (Matthew 3:2). This word *hand* is the Greek word *eggizo,* which means "approach, near." It's broken down to the word *eggus*, which means "to squeeze or throttle, or near in place or time, ready."

Jesus knew that if the man had enough faith to ask about eternal life and that there were eternal riches waiting for him, He knew that the man needed to be tested because he could only see what was in the earth realms. When Jesus offered him the option to sell everything, He was inviting him to see at a different level. He was inviting him to open the treasuries of Heaven to release what is in Heaven that would be his for eternity—it could all be released in the present moment and he would have more than enough.

Whether you're rich or poor, we all have access to eternal life and we all have access to the riches of Heaven. It does not matter where your faith level is. What do you believe to be true?

What is it that you understand to be true about Jesus and about eternal life? If you don't believe it's all there for you and accessible now, then you are living far less by faith than Jesus wants for you. This is a hard thing to grasp in our minds. We say, "Oh great, that's wonderful. That's in the afterlife. I'll have all that when I go to Heaven." No, it is a real truth in the moment, this moment.

Jesus was speaking to the rich young ruler about what was coming because Jesus hadn't died yet, hadn't yet broken the curse, the bondage of sin, death in the grave, the bondage of lack, the bondage of greed. He hadn't yet broken any of that. Jesus was speaking prophetically. "If you believe in me by faith as Messiah, you'll have all that. You don't need to worry about riches on earth, I give you access to heavenly treasuries through Me."

Do you know Jesus is your Lord and Savior? If yes, you have access to heavenly riches now through Jesus. That's good news!

In Luke 18:25 (NKJV), Jesus says, *"For it is easier for a camel to go through the eye of a needle than for a rich man to enter the kingdom of God."*

This scripture has been taken a lot of different ways. When we think about a sewing needle and a big fat camel fitting through a needle's eye, that's impossible. But that's not exactly what it means. The eye of a needle may be referring to rock formations in the part of the world where Jesus was speaking where camels traveled carrying people and goods from place to place. It was difficult for them to get through the narrow openings in the rocks.

Historically, some say the gates in the city walls were not high enough for camels to fit through, especially because of their humps. Either way, I believe this is a hyperbole statement, an exaggeration by Jesus, who was in essence saying, "You enter My Kingdom by faith. If you want the Kingdom of Heaven to be made manifest on earth you must believe in Me. I'm walking here on earth now. I bring the Kingdom with Me everywhere I go, wherever I am. This is what it is like to bring the Kingdom of Heaven to the earth. He said, "It's more impossible for a camel to go through an eye of the needle than for somebody who has so much to believe there is more waiting for them in Heaven."

That's what that means! You have more in Heaven, and you don't have to wait until you die because you have already entered eternity. The big lie of satan is that we can't enter into the full provision of the Garden of Eden now. This is a lie, Jesus has given us access back through the flaming sword at the edge of the Garden of Eden. Genesis 3:24 (NIV), *"After he drove the man out, he placed on the east side of the Garden of Eden cherubim and a flaming sword flashing back and forth to guard the way to the tree of life."*

And through Jesus's death, burial, resurrection, and ascension we have full access now to life eternal—not when we die and our body goes in the earth and our spirit and soul go to Heaven. This is the lie that is holding people in bondage daily. The lie that we have to wait. We are separated by our lack of faith, earth and Heaven, like a chasm still exists. No. Jesus has resurrected the earth so it is eternal in significance, time, and space, and we have now returned to living in the Garden—in the heavenly place of eternal and everlasting life. The time code has been cracked wide open.

When you became born again, that's when you entered eternity. In that moment, that moment of time, you entered eternal life. That means everything that is available in eternity is available to you. Now you must learn how to access it by faith and see.

Jesus was testing the rich young ruler when He told him he could live by faith that will cause him to enter the realms of the eternal; and with that, he would gain much more than he currently had. Jesus was prophesying, "When I go to the Cross and all this happens and I'm buried and resurrected, and we all go up, we're all ascended, you will have everything you need."

Do you believe what you're reading? I ask you now. Do you believe in the Word of God? Do you believe that when Jesus died, was buried, and resurrected that He defeated sin and death in the grave, and then He ascended? Do you believe that 40 days later He sent you the Holy Spirit, which is His Kingdom being made manifest on earth? Do you believe that you now have all access to the heavenly realm and everything in it?

There are no restrictions for you, absolutely no restrictions. You are without restrictions. No one is withholding anything from you. No one is stopping you from receiving what you need.

No devil is stopping your blessing from coming to you, in the name of Jesus. If you think in your soul (mind, will, and emotions) that lie is true, break it off right now. You must renew your mind. In the name of Jesus, we bind every enemy. God is trying to raise your level of faith to know that your pocketbook can be handed over in full in earth time and God will supply, from eternal realms today, all of your needs according to His glorious riches in Christ Jesus.

Where are your eyes looking? Are you always looking down at today's worries—or are you looking up, with *eido* covenant eyes, *anablepo* eyes to the abundant blessings available to you every day? I have more insights on the heavenly treasuries and the vats of Heaven in my book, *Releasing Heaven: Creating Supernatural Environments Through Heavenly Encounters.*

Wealthy Realms Are Now

God is doing a mighty thing. We are breaking strongholds off your mind. You have access to true riches and true wealth. You do not have to wait for access until you get to Heaven—all is yours now.

Now again, what do you believe? I am challenging you to think about what you believe and the lies of the enemy that may be binding you to the lie that you don't have access to heavenly riches now.

- Do you believe in the goodness of God?
- Do you believe that He loves you?
- Do you believe that He supplies all of your needs?

If there is a question in your heart in any way in regard to these three questions, it's time to repent. It's time to say, "Father, forgive me. I don't think I believe that and its fullness of truth. I think I'm supposed to do X and Y and Z because not all that I need is given to me at this moment." Listen, Jesus chose to give His people the Promised Land and He gave them everything they needed when they went from Egypt to the Promised Land—the same God who existed then exists today.

God gave us His Son, Jesus. He's giving you everything you need. Believe it.

You may think you need to work hard just to scrape by and you're doing all you can and it's all about you needing to receive from all your toiling. But as has been explained and proven throughout this book, it's time for a mind shift. It's not about how hard you work. It's about your faith in what Jesus has already worked out for you. It is true that there's natural laws and you have to sow and then you reap. *But* when you sow to the Spirit, you reap from the Spirit.

Galatians 6:7-9 (KJV) tells us:

> ***Be not deceived***; God is not mocked: for whatsoever a man soweth, that shall he also reap. For he that soweth

> to his flesh shall of the flesh reap corruption; but ***he that soweth to the Spirit shall of the Spirit reap life everlasting.*** And let us not be weary in well doing: for ***in due season we shall reap***, if we faint not.

This word *season* is the Greek word *kairos,* which means a set or proper time in the earth realms. Your blessings come from the fact that the earth time code has been cracked and that eternity is bringing forth all you need on earth at exactly the right time. Remember, earth time is condensed into eternal time. Eternal time has no beginning and no end. Earth's *kairos* time is included in that; and as time and space is moving, there will come a moment in earth time where all will be released—you just need to believe it.

> The Lord smelled the pleasing aroma and said in his heart: "Never again will I curse the ground because of humans, even though every inclination of the human heart is evil from childhood. And never again will I destroy all living creatures, as I have done. As long as the earth endures, seedtime and harvest, cold and heat, summer and winter, day and night will never cease" (Genesis 8:21-22 NIV).

In the days of Noah, when the flood ended, Jesus had not even come on the scene to meet the requirements of the Mosaic law. Yet God spoke of days on earth when blessings would come into earth time and that the ground would not have additional curses put on it. There would not be another rain coming in so much force to flood humanity out of existence, all except Noah and his family. Jesus came from the Davidic line that descended from Noah's lineage.

Harvest of Everlasting Realms

So when you sow to the everlasting realms, the everlasting realms have to bring forth the harvest in your life. Which means if you spend time trusting God and resting and making choices that are in alignment with believing in God's goodness and His love, you set yourself up for what that realm has to give you.

However, if you don't see it that way and live from a way not in alignment with God's way, you can't expect to receive. And that's what the story of the rich young ruler is all about.

> Indeed, it is easier for a camel to go through the eye of a needle than for someone who is rich to enter the kingdom of God." Those who heard this asked, "Who then can be saved?" Jesus replied, "What is impossible with man is possible with God" (Luke 18:25-27 NIV).

What we see as humans with our own eyesight, *blepo,* as impossible, God sees through spiritual eyes, our covenant with Him, as possible. Your impossibilities are limitations, restrictions, which is exactly what you need to recognize as simply opportunities or faith challenges to believe that the time code has been cracked and all is yours eternally—even if you don't see it in the earth realms yet. Your *kairos* from the earth realms has not yet reached your eternal time.

The reference of a camel going through the eye of a needle was for the young man to realize that his riches were like the eye of the needle, the things he was holding on to. The riches had become his identity. For many of us, our identity is in our work or what we do, it is in our gain. Is your identity in the things of the world and in how you work or toil within the curse of the fall? Or is your identity in the marvelous fact that you've been saved, healed, redeemed, and set apart by the shed blood of Jesus Christ?

Do you want a new identity? An identity that will never run out of the resources that are available to you? All you have to do is receive Jesus as your Lord and Savior. Just say, "Father, I confess my sin. I've been thinking it's all about me, how hard I work, how much I plot and scheme, how much I manipulate. I believe Jesus is the Son of God and He lived and died for my salvation, which I accept right now in His precious name."

It's okay if you didn't realize that was your identity. The enemy uses that against us, and the curse of the fall causes us to respond in our soul (mind, will, and emotions) to see life through the eyes of what we do. And sometimes we do what we don't want to do. Even the apostle Paul says, *"But what I hate I do"* (Romans 7:15 NIV). If there are things you do that you don't want to do, it is time to confess that.

Pray this prayer with me, "Lord, forgive me. I'm trying so hard. I'm so worn out. I'm busted. I'm disgusted. I'm burned out. Lord, I need Your help." Confession right now in the name of Jesus if this applies to you. I speak life over you right now that the Holy Spirit is coming into your room. Angels are coming into your room. Lord, we break strongholds off my reader friend right now, in the name of Jesus, and release Heaven upon Your beloved child.

I release the love of God to you. God loves you, son or daughter. You are a child of the King. He does not want you to toil anymore. Your heavenly Father wants you to till and step into the place of possibility with Him. Nothing is impossible with God. He wants you to step into that place. It may feel impossible for you, but it's possible with God—God does the impossible.

Faith Activation for Wealth Release

Now let's do a few faith activations. Grab every bill you owe this month and hold them up. These bills may be weighing you down—they may be overwhelming. You owe this and you owe that.

Hold them up to the Lord right now and we're going to break off that burden in the name of Jesus. God loves you and it's all paid. The bills are all paid in Jesus's name. I need you to believe that. I need you to sit before the Lord and say, "Lord, I thank You because You've paid every single one of these bills. Lord, You're helping me right now. You're showing me the way to move and believe in the new and living way, in the name of Jesus."

Receive His love. Receive His blessing. Receive His salvation. He doesn't want you to toil over this stuff you're faced with right now. We bind the enemy who comes to kill, steal, and destroy—and the enemy's curse is broken. Jesus broke it. Now it's time to step into the freedom that God is calling you to live in.

In the name of Jesus, put your hands out in front of you as if you're receiving silver and gold from Heaven. Receive all those bills paid. Let anxiety go. Believe you're seeing differently now. I see in the Spirit that you're seeing different. Angels are going to start giving you a new strategy. This strategy is by faith and faith alone. Everything that you bless, give away. Start thinking of how you are going to give some stuff away. Give some clothes out of your closet. Give away some food. Give things away that you don't need but others do need.

Giving will start portals of blessings to open for you. Heavenly portals will open on your behalf. I'm prophesying to you in the mighty name of Jesus that every bill is taken care of right now. You're going to receive phone calls. You're going to go to your mailbox. You will receive what you need. Good things are happening now.

Jesus is the great I AM and He is the One who created everlasting time. He invites us to learn to live in this place daily. This is a time and season when as Kingdom citizens we must know how to defy the effects of death, of earth time, and step into the realities of eternal time. Let's make decisions from this special place as long as it is *today.*

12

Nothing Can Stop You Now

To fully step into supernatural acceleration, stop cycles of delay, and secure God's promises, we must understand the essence of cracking the time code. The time code is knowing the differences between earth time and eternal time. Understanding that earth time is within a continuum of what is completed already and written already in earth time.

Jesus cracked the time code for you on earth by His selfless death, burial, resurrection, and ascension. Now all things have been redeemed on earth, and you are at one with eternal time. This means that although sometimes you operate out of conforming to the pattern of this world, as apostle Paul says you will *"be transformed by the renewing of your mind"* (Romans 12:2 NIV).

We must understand that the fall of man and its curse was the power of death to hold us in a state of bondage, which we process the world through "getting" and not "giving." In our sin and depravity, we had to have broken our lack and sinful desires to gain provision, protection, and acceptance—to be catapulted into a new life as givers. God is the ultimate Giver, and we as His sons and daughters must be too.

Yes there is scientific, biblical, and historical understanding of cracking the time code; and when we can live it out daily in this space of fullness of life and giving, we are living out the effects of being redeemed. This is how we are to be today, members of earth time who now have an endless life. We have defeated sin, death, and the grave because all that Jesus has done for us has been credited to us in righteousness.

Final Thoughts

As you exit this book, I want to empower you with these final thoughts. You are free and no longer a slave to sin and death. You are free to be a giver. Once you grasp that all of the Bible is about learning to break the habits of the curse of the fall of man and what death or lack of time has done to humanity through the lies of satan, the truth will set you free and now you can live in the Promised Land. Nothing can stop you now.

The key to fully cracking the time code is to live as a giver by faith. Everything will challenge you otherwise. God causes us to live by faith as it is what pleases Him (Hebrews 11:6). He rewards those who live by faith and who endeavor to rest in faith (Hebrews 4). We must understand in cracking the time code that faith is necessary.

Romans 14:23 (NIV) says, *"...everything that does **not** come from **faith** is sin."*

Jesus revealed how faith works on earth. How faith itself can defeat earth time. He believed and He obeyed His Father. Hebrews 5:7-8 (NKJV) says:

> In the days of His flesh, when He had offered up prayers and supplications, with vehement cries and

> tears to Him who was able to save Him from death, and was heard because of His godly fear, though He was a Son, yet He learned obedience by the things which He suffered.

By our faith in Jesus we are overcomers of death and we defeat time constraints. He in His suffering made it possible for us to enter the new eternal order of Melchizedek and now we as a church are called to live having defeated sin, death, and the grave, which is the essence of cracking the time code daily by our own faith. From here we enter His rest and open faith portals to wealth and prosperity of soul and the riches of Heaven being made manifest to us, His people.

God is calling us to be givers in faith. It takes faith to live by every word that proceeds out of the mouth of the Lord. It takes faith to fall within the boundary lines of what God is telling us to do. It takes faith to subdue our flesh and not conform to the pattern of this world and to be renewed to a new pathway of being a giver. The release of wealth comes easily when our mindset is already as a giver and we believe in the riches and treasures of heavenly wealth, like the challenge of the rich young ruler. God's ways are that of giving, and when we use up our resources by faith, He gives us more.

Jesus tell us in Luke 6:38 (NIV), *"Give, and it will be given to you. A good measure, pressed down, shaken together and running over, will be poured into your lap. For with the measure you use, it will be measured to you."*

The reason giving can be hard is because of fear. We live under a curse or lie that our resources are small or limited. When we begin to feel like we don't have enough, then we fall under the curse of the fall of man and that positions us to try to gain. It is a terrible cycle of death and unbelief—exactly where satan wanted Adam and Eve and all of humanity. But by faith all we have to do is remember that Jesus gave it all that we might now be givers. If we live within that supernatural space of being givers, we will begin to receive the manifestation of the Garden of Eden, or the Promised Land. This is our inheritance as sons and daughters who live seated with Christ in heavenly places.

This manifestation comes from believing they had all things, all the time, everywhere in the presence of the Lord and they simply gave one to another. It was the enemy that came to cause them to be "getters" instead of "givers." Now we enter His rest and are redeemed from the toil of our labor, and we are now properly positioned by faith in a full Garden. Now we can give all we have received through what Jesus has done as the Giver of His own life and by receiving the power of the Holy Spirit. See, now you can do it.

If you get nothing from this book, please get this:

First, that the curse of the fall man has been broken. Time has been redeemed. You've been made complete, whole in full. You've received all things and are now positioned in the Garden of Eden in a new eternal Kingdom order of Melchizedek, and now your job is to be a giver, and to open yourself to the supernatural release of all the resources of Heaven. Yes, now you can give and give beyond measure because, *"**Freely** you have **received; freely give**"* (Matthew 10:8 NIV).

Let this be your motto: *I have freely received, so I will now freely give of my time, talent, treasure, and testimony—because I live in the Promised Land today!*

This confession of faith means you will be living as though time and all the effects of death have been redeemed. Now you can do it! You are living with a new eternal time code!

Prayer of Faith

I want to pray for you right now.

> *Dear Lord, thank You for my friend who is seeking to live in the eternal time zone. This reader is seeking to be intimate with You from the understanding they are seated with You in heavenly places, and in the realm of faith of the ascension realms. I thank You, Father, that You are now opening realms of understanding, wisdom, and revelation that will be keys to crack the time code for this friend's own life.*
>
> *We thank You that You did the final cracking of the time code; now all we must do is to live as though we have an endless life and we are properly positioned in heavenly places and earthly spaces where the new eternal Kingdom order of Melchizedek has been accomplished. Activate our spiritual gifts and a boldness to go and live complete and finished.*

* * *

If you are reading this and have not received Jesus as your Lord and Savior, it is time to do that now. Simply confess that you need a Savior and that Jesus is the One. Confess any sin to the Lord or underlying issues that you may have. Ask Him for forgiveness and you will be forgiven. Romans 10:9-13 (NIV) says:

> If you declare with your mouth, "Jesus is Lord," and believe in your heart that God raised him from the dead, you will be saved. For it is with your heart that you believe and are justified, and it is with your mouth that you profess your faith and are saved. As Scripture

> says, "Anyone who believes in him will never be put to shame." For there is no difference between Jew and Gentile—the same Lord is Lord of all and richly blesses all who call on him, for, "Everyone who calls on the name of the Lord will be saved."

There is so much more I can teach you about cracking the time code, supernatural wealth, and the culture of Heaven. I invite you to reach out to me at www.candicesmithyman.com or www.dreammentors.org. I encourage you to take some of my classes or become part of my apostolic network of biblical life and transformational life coaches. Maybe God is calling you today to advance His Kingdom ministry by helping yourself and others. We want to bless you.

ABOUT CANDICE SMITHYMAN

Dr. Candice Smithyman is an international apostolic and prophetic revivalist and healing minister. She is founder of Dream Mentors International, a global, biblical life-coaching and transformational life-coaching institute.

Candice is also host of the *Glory Road* television broadcast that showcases international prophetic voices and can be seen on Faith USA, UK, and Africa, PTL Network, King TV, Praise TV, and Precious TV, which all minister to Muslim populations and the poorest nations in the world via satellites and other outlets.

Dr. Smithyman is host of *Your Path to Destiny* on Sid Roth's It's Supernatural Network (ISN). She also hosts the *On the Glory Road* podcast with Destiny Image Publishers, and *Manifest His Presence* podcast with *Charisma Magazine*. Candice has been a guest on Sid Roth's *It's Supernatural,* as well as *Today with Marilyn and Sarah, The Paula White Today Show,* and many others.

Contact Information

Websites
candicesmithyman.com
www.dreammentors.org
Email: info@candicesmithyman.com
Candice Smithyman Ministries
PO Box 65656
Orange Park, FL 32065